THE LAW OF BRAND ATTRACTION 2

27 Inspired Thought Leaders
From The Visionary Hub
Plus Dr John Demartini From The Secret
Share Their Best Advice On How To
Build A Magnetic Global Movement
Around The Gifts And Talents
YOU ALREADY HAVE

www.thelawofbrandattraction.com

The Law Of Brand Attraction 2

First published in April 2021 WM Publishing

ISBN 978-1-912774-90-6 (e-book)
ISBN 978-1-912774-91-3 (pbk)

Editors: Sammy Blindell, Andrew Priestley

A CIP catalogue record for this book is available from the British Library.

Contents

Foreword By Dr John Demartini

The Law of Brand Attraction Turning Your Greatest Setbacks Into Your Greatest Comebacks

Have you ever experienced what you initially thought was a great setback and sooner or later received a great lesson?

It may even have been a comeback and the experience turned out to be on the way, not in the way. Perhaps you have experienced many lessons in this manner, and you could fill an entire book with your own stories! Maybe one of those great lessons changed the course of your entire life.

Whatever challenges you experience in life, you have the power to transform them into your greatest opportunities and even your legacy - starting now.

I have had the opportunity to learn many great lessons throughout my life, particularly along my career path, a few of which I'd love to share with you here as you embark on your inspiring journey of transforming your inner dream into an outer visionary business through reading this book.

One early setback, opportunity and lesson that came to mind occurred when I was just 17 years old. I had previously dropped out of middle school because I had learning difficulties and was living in a tent on the North Shore of Oahu Hawaii as a surfer.

I had a close brush with death. It was a really challenging time and I was not sure if I was going to make it. I was in dire need of a change and inspiration when one night I met a gentleman named Paul C Bragg, who happened to be lecturing at a sunset recreation hall nearby. It was as if my prayers had been answered as he literally changed my life with one simple message in one hour for me.

His presentation inspired me to believe that I could someday overcome my learning challenges and become intelligent, and that I'd be able to read, write and speak effectively. I'm grateful and delighted to say since that night, with determination I learned how to read, write and speak effectively - which I have done consistently to this day. Since then, many setbacks and challenges have become great lessons and opportunities. For instance:

Lesson one: You are always in the right place at the right time to meet the right teacher.

If you have somehow picked up this book, I would encourage you to consider letting this book be your next great right teacher.

Paul C Bragg became one of my earlier great right teachers, and I was eager to learn more from him. After I spent a few weeks studying with him each morning, he told me, "John, you have a body, you have a mind, and you have a soul. Your body must be directed by your mind and your mind must be directed by your soul in order to maximize your human potential and become unstoppable."

I started doing the action steps he taught me. I started to take command of what I thought, what I saw, what I felt about myself, how I talked to myself and what actions I took.

He gave me a little affirmation after I told him I had learning problems. He said, "John, I want you to say to yourself every single day, *I'm a genius and I apply my wisdom*." I've never missed a day in nearly 49 years now. I just never gave up on my dream.

Lesson two: If you have a clear and inspiring vision in your mind, a calling in your heart and a message that can deeply and meaningfully impact the world, it is wise to keep persevering no matter what. Let there be no turning back.

I began memorizing 30 words a day out of a dictionary and eventually learned that I could actually read incrementally and begin to comprehend. I discovered that I could retain and express what I learned if I expressed it immediately afterwards. I then became unstoppable. Learning has since then gone from being one of the most challenging experiences of my life to one of the most invigorating, inspiring aspects of my life, and I still read voluminously today. In fact, I have made it my mission to fill my mind with the greatest teachings I can learn from the greatest minds whoever lived from around the world. I then disseminate that information as quickly and effectively as I can, just like we are doing right now in this inspiring book.

Lesson three: As a visionary business owner with a movement calling you to step up, this third and final lesson is one of the most important you can learn within your brand attraction strategy. It's the Universal Law of the 'One to Many', which can be applied to absolutely everything!

"What is it?" I hear you ask.

Let me explain...

Imagine you're walking down the street and you meet somebody whom you look up to and admire. You're attracted to them, but you're too humble to admit that what you see in them is inside you. You assume they have something you don't, so you disown what you see in them and you deflect it. In the process of doing that, you put them on a pedestal, and you put yourself in a pit. You exaggerate them towards an expansion, and you minimize yourself towards a contraction.

Now imagine that you meet somebody whom you look at and

despise and look down upon. You resent them, but you're too proud to admit that what you see in them is inside you.

Now you put them down and shrink them, while expanding pride in yourself.

These two scenarios emerge from an inequity of perception.

The moment you infatuate or resent any another individual, and put them above or below you, and make them greater or lesser than you, they automatically begin to occupy space and time in your mind and your misperception of them will begin to run you. When you're infatuated or resentful, you're conscious of their upsides/downsides and unconscious to their downsides/upsides. The moment you have such a conscious and unconscious split, you divide your mind from one into many. You disempower yourself and put your personas on, which are masks, such as your minimized shame or exaggerated pride mask.

These aren't you. These are false personas of you; the facades that you cover your authentic self with. The moment you do that, you disempower yourself because you're disowning parts of yourself.

You want to be loved for who you are, but if you are not willing to be who you are, how are they going to be able to? The truth is you have everything within you – nothing is missing. You're both the hero and the villain. You're the saint and the sinner. You have virtue and you have vice. So putting other people up or down instead of putting them in your heart is only going to split you up and disempower you.

By using the Universal Law of the One to Many, you are going within, reclaiming and owning all your disowned parts. When you own all your parts, you level the playing field. You're not above or below people, you now have equanimity and objectivity. You're seeing things for the whole not the parts. You're empowered to transcend what you were judging. Every area of your life is affected when you create that judgment split and it is healed by your ability to own all the parts and return to your one authentic self or being.

When you see things in a perfect balance around you and within, you access the hidden order in your apparent chaos.

Whoever has the most order is the one that gives the orders, they're the leaders, the ones who have the most certainty.

But the second you subjective bias and distort your reality with conscious and unconscious splits or judgments, you automatically become run from extrinsic sources which can exhaust you, instead of being intrinsically called towards your primary objective or purpose in life, which is invigorating. That's why your primary objective, purpose or mission in life provides you with your path for mastery and legacy. Instead of being a victim of your history, you become a master of your destiny.

As the current brand leader of your social movement, there has never been a more critical time for you to step up and own every part of your being as an authentic individual and a leader. The world is waiting for you to step up and own and exemplify your whole authentic identity. It is essential for you to own your true and whole value and the many unique gifts and talents with which you were born, so that you can, in turn, embrace and own the impact you were put on this planet to make.

Within this book, you will find many lifetimes of lessons, all of which have been unpacked in a way to encourage and empower you to live your most authentic life in accordance with your highest values and most inspiring mission. When you live congruently with who you truly are, you have the highest probability of awakening your brain's executive centre and emerge as an impactful leader. When you take actions that are high in your list of values, or true priorities, your self-worth goes up. When you do things low on your list of values, your self-worth goes down. So if you would love to raise your self-worth, you would be wise to live by priority and make your highest priority the path of expressing who you are.

Trying to be someone you are not isn't the wisest way to rise to the top in life. Being second at being somebody else is not the wisest way to emerge as a true leader or rise. Minimizing or exaggerating yourself is more likely to result in you being a victim of your history, not a master of your destiny. So if you have found yourself at a point in your life where you want to know what your next wisest step is, you already have it within your heart and hands, and it is your highest priority in the moment.

This book is packed with solid advice on how to own your true identity, and your unique value, gift, impact and path, along with your specific brand and business strategy.

You'll learn exactly what to do with your newly transformed mindset and how to create or attract everything you want in your life through building a movement you are completely in love with!

In the process, you'll meet an extraordinary collection of authors who are absolutely here to serve you with the benefit of their experience, and their whole hearts.

You hold your future in your hands. What you do with it is now up to you.

May you have great fulfilment doing what you love and loving what you do as an inspired authentic leader, manifesting your most meaningful and impactful visionary dreams!

Dr John Demartini

International bestselling author of The Values Factor.

www.drdemartini.com

About Dr John Demartini

Dr John Demartini is a world-renowned, award-winning, specialist in human behavior, a researcher, international bestselling author, consultant, and global educator who has presented in 154 countries for the last 48 years.

As founder of the Demartini Research and Education Institute, he has developed and trademarked a series of methodological solutions to human conditions applicable across most markets, sectors and age groups. He has been interviewed on thousands of radio and television talk shows, as well as social media platforms, webinars and podcasts.

His articles and interviews have regularly appeared in over 1,500 magazines and newspapers worldwide and he has starred in over 30 movies or film documentaries. His audiences and clientele have ranged from leaders of governments, corporations, and entrepreneurs, to university educators, celebrities, and sports personalities.

Contact Dr John Demartini

www.drdemartini.com

Launch Your Ripple, Make Your Wave!

Sammy Blindell - The Ripple Maker

"People will buy into your vision when your life backs up the words you say."

"Oh my gosh Sammy, you've got to buy it," said my friend Lynn as we stood at the checkout of this cute little store.

We are window shopping whilst waiting to fly back to London after filming a documentary together in San Diego. I've seen a beautiful teardrop-shaped pendant and nudged Lynn excitedly exclaiming, "Look Lynn, it's a One Drop!"

After encouraging me to buy it, she looks at me blankly and asks what a One Drop is?

"Everyone knows what a One Drop is, don't they?" I say confidently. From the look on her face, it turns out the One Drop Impact Code I have built all seven of my successful businesses on is not well-known at all!

The reality is, I have been a One Drop for so long that I've taken its value for granted, not even seeing its gift anymore. I hadn't seen the value it could be to others as I thought it was something everyone does anyway. The penny dropped! Being a One Drop silently isn't enough any longer. If I am going to own my impact, I must **own my identity** around it, **own the value** I can bring through it, **own the gifts** I have mastered while doing it and **own my lane** by stepping into the power of it.

What gifts are you currently sat on that you haven't been telling enough people about yet?

I realised that being a One Drop is a gift. This gift was crying for attention so blatantly it was almost leaping out of me. I had been ignoring this calling long enough and it was no longer going to hide silently inside me.

What calling do you have in your heart that is silently (or perhaps loudly) crying out to be birthed?

No matter how much you ignore it, your purpose will find a way to make you listen. I have a feeling this book is in your hands for exactly that reason!

The One Drop story, like your story, has waited to be birthed long enough. It's a story packed with lessons you should know before you devour all the goodies that we are about to share with you in this book. You'll have to come back to a very cold December evening in 2002 though for me to show you how it all started...

I'm sitting in a room full of start-up businesses waiting for the presenter to walk on stage. It's an evening course I enrolled in to learn about accounting for the new business I'd set up the week before. I literally know nothing about business at this point and want to soak up everything I can learn to get started the right way first time. The presenter steps onto the stage, giving us a lovely warm welcome when he flicks his screen to the welcome slide of his presentation. My eyes are immediately glued to the words on the big blue screen in front of me.

'Individually, we are one drop. Together we are an ocean.'
Ryunosuke Satoro

I'm looking at those words wondering what they mean?

What does it mean to be a one drop? Can anyone be a one drop? Am I a one drop? How do we all become a one drop? How do we become an ocean? What would I have to do to be a one drop? My mind is racing as I imagine everyone in this room being a one drop together like an ocean.

Is he a one drop?

Is she a one drop?

I look inquisitively at each and every face in the room.

My imagination is in overdrive as I think about how each of these people could make a positive ripple that creates a wave - potentially reaching the whole world.

"Wow! Just imagine that!" I think to myself. "If each of these 23 people make a positive ripple of impact, we could make the whole world of difference. What if everyone in the world lived life this way? Imagine the impact we can make if everyone lives as a one drop."

Suddenly, one drop becomes One Drop on my notepad. My movement (I have no idea in this moment it's a movement yet) claims its name and I silently become a Ripple Maker!

The next hour is a blur as I note all the thoughts and ideas that flow through me straight into my notepad. It's as if the Universe said, Finally guys, she's got it. Load her up!

I started thinking about all the people who have created a ripple of impact in my life. I think about how grateful I am to my mum for being the best demonstration of her gift by bringing communities together wherever she goes. I think about how grateful I am to my dad for joining our little family of two when I was just three years old, bringing me up with so much love as his own daughter. *Definite Ripple Makers*, I nod to myself!

I think about my grandma and the ripple of impact she made while she was alive. *She was definitely One Drop*, I note. People would travel from faraway places to come and be healed by her. I'd watch them slump into her kitchen, wincing in pain and walk out practically skipping in delight! They always wanted to pay her, but she never took a penny from them. She just asked them to put money in her bright little tin on top of the fridge and everything in it would go to her favourite charities when full.

I always wanted to be like her - a gracious, grateful and generous miracle worker with an infectious giggle. She could have you in tears of laughter without even knowing what you were laughing at. Elsie May was loved by everyone who knew her because of how she showed up for you as if you were the only person in the world.

I wonder what my business would be like if I become One Drop, adopting grandma's essence into everything I do? I write it in my notepad. It feels so right. From this moment on, if something doesn't measure up to these core principles, I won't do it. I write.

My One Drop Impact Code proudly becomes:

Graceful Grateful Generous

I write a mantra that I silently repeat to myself three times every morning from that day on to start my day the One Drop way, *Please guide me to be the greatest ripple maker I can be for others today, I say before I open my eyes.*

This mantra becomes something I do daily for the next sixteen years, right up to the moment I stood in that store with Lynn in 2018, telling her about One Drop. I realise that my biggest successes have been when I ticked all of those Impact Code principles. All the things that had gone wrong were things I did without running them through my Impact Code filter first. Bam!

The greatest lesson you can learn before you get stuck into this book is this - when you finally commit to the movement that's calling you from within, you will gather momentum quickly. Once you know the what, you'll find that the *who* and the *how* show up perfectly timed!

For example, I wanted to create a global symbol for One Drop Movement and knew the drop was going to become the ONE united symbol that would represent One Drop.

I had no idea how I was going to make that happen, but after telling my mum (an incredibly talented glass designer) what I wanted to do, she volunteered to create the perfect 'drop'. After 11 months of daily experimentation, she made a beautiful, luminescent, One Drop unity pendant and keyring that our Ripple Makers now wear with pride as we create a united world through collaborative partnerships. Thirty percent of every sale goes to the charities we support, enabling us to give back as we *Drop it Forward* and grow the global movement. The *who* and the *how* showed up!

Just like my story of One Drop Movement, when you start to own your gifts, own your value and get a taste of the impact you can make with your ripple, you will want to increase that impact faster. I know this will happen to you because it happened to me and it happens to every one of our Ripple Makers!

To increase our ripple of impact, for example, we started running monthly Brand Accelerators in a Facebook group for our Ripple Makers around the world to continue growing their movements.

Over time it became a fun five-day festival called RippleFEST that we now deliver every month for our Ripple Makers and their friends. We raise thousands for charity every month through our collective Quest, whilst raising hundreds of brands from the ground up. In fact, every person you are going to get to know throughout this book is part of the RippleFEST Quest, so make sure you come by and meet us all at the Quest some time!

Now, my friend, you are ready to go. You already have your One Drop inside you and this book will take you step by step through the process of shaping it, owning it, valuing it, packaging it and then sharing it with the world.

The power is literally in your hands right now to be the ripple you wish to see in the world.

So let's be that One Drop together and commit to creating a Ripple of Impact greater than any other that came before us.

I believe in you, so let's do this.

With love,

Sammy xx

About Sammy Blindell

Sammy is a multi-award-winning international speaker, seven times best-selling author, CEO of Brand Builders Club and Founder of the One Drop Movement.

After 13 years in branding before building her first five businesses, Sammy burned out putting profit before purpose. She left it all to follow her 'Ripple of Impact' vision, building her first online program and brand building resource in 2014. Within 12 weeks she was making £18,000 + per month, followed by other programmes that enabled Sammy to build significant wealth before turning 40.

In February 2017, she launched Brand Builders Club, followed by her global movement 'One Drop' in April 2019, to unite one million change-makers through collaborative global partnerships.

Sammy has since created 80+ online programmes and 1000+ online courses, showing others how to create their Ripple of Impact in just a few months. She's now on a mission to share how you can do it too.

Contact Sammy Blindell

sociatap.com/sammyblindell

Part One

Own Your IDENTITY

Born Free...
When Life Gets In The Way, It's Time To Come Home To Your S.O.U.L.

Deborah FreeSpirit -The Heart-Centered SOUL Synergist

"Life challenges are your greatest teachers, because other people's weaknesses will enable you to come home to your S.O.U.L."

As I sit on the floor of another cold, strange place, I cradle my legs and stare blindly into the distance. My tear-stained face feels tight with anguish and my heart is pounding. My 60th birthday is just a few weeks away, but I don't feel like celebrating. How selfish I am? I thought to myself. Anyone else would be celebrating their life, but here I am working out how I'm going to end it. Suicide felt like my only option. That day would become what I lovingly refer to as *my dark night of the soul.*

As I saw the movie of my life running through my mind, my stomach churned with memories of me as a little girl in Kenya. She was born with lioness energy, afraid of nothing and nobody. Then, at five years old, her whole life crashed down around her. I recall it like it was yesterday.

Dad has come home drunk again, but this time it's different. The night before, it's my sister's birthday party and he's drunk in front of the family. He smashes the birthday cake on the floor, and I hear him and mum arguing... again. Mum is upset, she picks me up and tells my older sister, "Get ready, we're leaving."

Dad grabs my sister. I'm so scared, tired and confused. I run towards mum and we quickly run towards the door.

As we run through it, mum realises my sister is still in the house with him and panics. She reaches for my sister, but her arm gets caught in the doorway. Dad slams the door shut, eventually letting my sister go and we run onto the street. A kind neighbour alerts my uncle, who comes to pick us up. But as we wait for him scared and vulnerable in the street, mum sobs. Her arm is broken, and we are now homeless... for the first time.

We find a home eventually. It's a big shed at the back of a house, which we rent. It's one room with a bunk bed; my sister on the top, then mum and I on the bottom. We have a tiny kitchen, a separate toilet and a shower outside with only cold water.

Three years on, mum tells us we are moving to England with her friend, Uncle Ernest. Mum's in love, but I don't trust him. Mum reassures me everything will be OK, but my gut says *it's never going to be OK.*

On the flight to London, Uncle Ernest gets drunk and makes a scene on the flight. On arrival at Heathrow airport, police are waiting to question Uncle Ernest. I am so embarrassed, I wish the ground would open up and swallow me. We're in a new country, and my 10-year-old self-wishes to be back in Kenya.

Now aged 14, mum has married Uncle Ernest, who is now my stepfather. His narcissistic behaviour impacts all my teenage years, and it takes mum another four years to realise it's too late. She's allowed another abuser into her life.

The atmosphere at home is chilly, and there's an unusual silence in the room next door. "Something is going down tonight" I tell my sister. I can't hear anything, not even the television. "This definitely isn't right", I say, and we walk into mum's room to find my stepdad with his Kashmiri ceremonial knife held against mum's throat. My sister calms him down and I pull mum away, but the knife slips and there is blood everywhere.

Neighbours alert the police, and six officers charge up the stairs as they arrive on the scene. Two of them handcuff my stepfather to take him away, while the others check we are okay. They take mum to the hospital and we pack our things – this time we're heading to a safe house.

Homeless again. I'm feeling lost, deflated and confused. We're not allowed to tell anyone where we are staying, so I lose my friends, my identity and the life I'd finally started to build.

As my life movie flashes through my mind, I come back to reality on that floor. I realise my identity is still that little girl with lioness energy, afraid of nothing and nobody. Then it hit me! I can continue to let other people define my identity, my security and my life, or I can come home to myself and live my life by design. I'm delighted to tell you personally that I chose to live!

Six months after my 60th birthday, my Higher Self tells me, *Deborah, I'm so proud of you. You're a free spirit, and you've always been. Welcome home, dear one. Your soul has been set free. It's time to sparkle and share your story with the world.*

I've spent a lot of time visualising since then, which enabled me to create a better life for myself and others. I took my skills to another level when I trained as a Law of Attraction teacher, giving me the secrets to manifestation that I now use more profoundly.

Join me now in a guided visualisation to come home to yourself and create your own sacred space. I use this sacred space to enter into meditations, daydreams, or write my journal. My Higher Self is the only other person allowed in this space.

I recommend you use 432Hz music as you prepare to create and enter your sacred space. You can find this on YouTube.

Start by finding yourself somewhere quiet where you will not be disturbed.

Choose to lie down or sit up. Make sure you are comfortable, with a blanket to hand in case you need it.

When you are ready, take three deep breaths. As you inhale and exhale, feel this beautiful white light frequency coming in through the top of your crown, sweeping through your entire body to create a wave of calmness.

The more you relax, the deeper you'll go.

Now see yourself standing in a beautiful forest surrounded by nature, with only the sound of birds chirping and the flow of a river nearby. You resonate with this place in your heart.

Ahead of you is a footpath. Follow the trail, observing what's around you. The further you walk, you notice a sign, 'Secret Garden'. In the distance, you see a golden footbridge.

As you walk across the footbridge, someone is walking towards you; it's your future Self, waiting patiently to welcome you with a big warm hug. You are handed a golden key, a gift which unlocks two doors.

You walk towards the Secret Garden and see a big wooden door. It leads you into an elevator. Press the button to open the door. Once you've entered, press the button 'U', which takes you to the lowest level. As you exit, follow the footpath to the second door.

Use the golden key again to open the door. After entering, the door automatically shuts behind you. You are inside an amethyst cave and can feel it's powerful calming energies. You walk around, discovering more and more things.

There's a glass door, which leads you onto a beautiful white sandy beach with a clear bluey/green lagoon leading to the ocean. The sand is soft and silky under your feet. You've never seen anything quite like it before. You run towards the water; the waves are calm and gentle. It feels like a warm bath.

Sitting down on the sand, you make yourself comfortable, soaking up all the magic of this place. The birds chirp away, singing you a song. You reflect on how lucky you are to have found this place.

You return to the cave. You see, hidden in the corner, a big comfortable chair with a bookcase full of all your favourite books. The sound of water is coming from behind the chair. It's a natural waterfall inside the cave and the perfect space to do your meditation. You sit comfortably in the big chair, ready to close your eyes and you start meditating.

You can come back to this sacred space whenever you feel you need to meditate, journal, daydream, or be alone.

When you are ready to leave the cave, walk back to the door. Follow the passage and enter the elevator pressing 'ML' to return to the main level.

As you exit the big wooden door of the cave, you find yourself back on the footpath. Your future Self is at the golden footbridge and shares words of advice and wisdom before giving you a big loving hug.

What did your future Self say to you? Write it down so you reflect on it.

Now, walk across the golden footbridge until you get to where you started.

As you come out of this meditation, take a deep in-breath. Gently and slowly open your eyes, giving your body time to adjust. You are complete.

Simply guide yourself back into this meditation to come home to yourself at any time and remember... your Higher Self ALWAYS has your back.

About Deborah FreeSpirit

Deborah FreeSpirit is an Advanced EFT Practitioner, Life Coach, International Law of Attraction Coach, Independent Angelic-Reiki Master, and Shamanic Practitioner. She's also a Licensed Practitioner in Saraswati Healing™, a unique soul healing and spiritual empowerment process.

In the early 1990s, Deborah discovered Usui Reiki, which piqued her interest to learn more so she could use her gifts to provide support and spiritual awakening for others.

In 2017, Deborah received clear guidance to embark on a soul journey. With a one-way ticket, she visited sacred sites in Egypt, Thailand, Malaysia, Bali, New Zealand, America, Jordan, Israel, Scotland, and Portugal. Deborah met, trained, and worked with Hopi elders in Arizona, and Māori teachers in New Zealand. She also supported her Māori teacher in Brisbane.

With 35 years of experience, Deborah has become a sought-after spiritual mentor with clients spanning the globe, supporting them through coaching, soul guidance readings, and healing sessions.

Contact Deborah FreeSpirit

http://www.deborahfreespirit.com

https://www.facebook.com/deborahfreespirit2020/

http://instagram.com/deborah_freespirit

http://linkedin.com/in/serenity4all

Who Are You?
Living Without Labels

Dee Twentyman - The Superconscious Collaborator

"If you don't learn to challenge your limited thinking, your thinking will challenge your life and everything in it."

On a cold wet morning, a timid, shy and embarrassed, eight-year-old me stood in the doctor's surgery looking down at the floor while my mum told the doctor that I can't go to the toilet. I was mortified. The more my mother told this stranger, the more I wanted that floor to swallow me up and the world to end.

This GP was ahead of his time and informed my mum that my condition was most likely a result of anxiety. I was forced to spill the beans right there and then. Embarrassingly, I admitted I'd been dragging my feet every morning and was making excuses to avoid school altogether. My desperate plea to avoid the bullying that was going on there. I was too ashamed to speak up for myself. Mum was told to *keep an eye on me.* That meant noticing my mood and make sure I was OK.

Mum did her best but couldn't do much with the three of us to bring up while working to make ends meet. She was busy keeping the wolf from the door, so I was left to cope with the anxiety and symptoms on my own.

Fifteen years later and there I was, planning my days and shopping trips around where the nearest public toilets were, just in case I needed to *go*. The meticulous planning was exhausting. I'd avoid certain stores knowing they would be full of people and I might have to jump out of a queue before getting to the cashier. I avoided public transport and anything that meant I might need the loo. My gut was controlling my life!

I was relying heavily on various pills when my IBS flared up, especially when I fell off the wagon. I still wanted to have fun with friends on night's out, but even an enjoyable meal meant spending ages choosing what to wear in case my stomach blew out like a balloon. I'd end up feeling sick and in excruciating pain. It was easier not to go out because I didn't want to spoil the night. I felt it just wasn't worth it and missed out on a lot. That became the story of my life!

I began looking into the foods that could trigger a bout of IBS and started my journey with natural wellbeing. No packaged foods, additives and everything cooked from scratch. I knew about the foods that harm and the foods that heal and found ways to *manage*. I got on with life, putting up with things that were uncomfortable thinking this is just how I am, an IBS sufferer. Even though I felt I had a handle on the foods that triggered me, I'd still have bouts of IBS symptoms and couldn't fathom why.

Pain medication had been a regular feature of my life for the next 20 or so years. Side effects were just as bad, if not worse, than the symptoms they were meant to relieve. I had to do something, and by the time I was in my thirties I was single with two daughters, a full-time job and a mortgage to pay. I found myself talking to a counsellor, looking at my life, wondering why on earth it appeared like I was managing but feeling pretty rotten a lot of the time.

Then, I remembered that cold morning in the doctor's surgery with mum being told I was an *anxious child*. A-ha! Something went ping inside my brain and I realised it was my gut speaking to me. I was emotionally out of line with my desires, wants and needs, and as if that wasn't enough, I was 23 years old when migraines began tagging along for the ride. I had managed the physical side of health and wellness, but one thing I'd missed was my thinking!

Everything I thought and felt about myself came from my past. My thoughts, feelings, assumptions, beliefs and labels! I wore these like some badge of honour for still carrying on, and *coping*! It was time for change, time to live life without the IBS label and take action in a positive direction.

After many years of training, certifications and treating people through my own programmes, I stepped up to set up my own business and qualify as a Hypno-Psychotherapist, specialising in the treatment of IBS and chronic pain. On my journey, I met so many people like me, looking to deal with their symptoms, not just manage them. I realised that I could help thousands of people around the world to change their lives just by owning my identity and sharing my story. Now my business is more than a business. It's a global movement and I am owning my identity in a global way for the first time.

Perhaps you have lived with a label that no longer serves you?

Maybe you can feel the calling to turn your greatest adversities into your greatest legacies.

If you are ready to take your next steps and really go for it, here are some tips I give my clients when they are starting out on their new journey.

Realign

Think differently. Many thinking styles will either take you toward owning your identity or move you away from it. Are you a negative thinker, assuming the worst? Do you obsess for weeks after an event? Maybe you catastrophise? Or are you a positive thinker, always seeing the best in every situation? Just be mindful to catch any negative thoughts and turn them into positive ones before they manifest physically into negative results. Remember, your thoughts become things!

Empower

Evaluate where you are now. Think about where you place control in your life. Is it internal, where you believe you determine what happens in your life? Or is it External, where you believe it's down to luck, fate or the weather? Internal control empowers you and means you won't quit before you get ahead.

Life Change

Recognise your BS! By that, I mean your Belief System! Think about the limitations of having to be perfect, believing you don't have the resources to move forward, or I'm not being good enough, Understanding how your BS feeds into your struggles gives you huge insights into why you have these limitations showing up in your life. If these struggles are showing up in your life, they are definitely going to start showing up in your business.

Intention

Set your end goals. Visualise yourself in the future as the new you and feel what it's like to go there. It's a great way to set an intention and see yourself achieving it. Top athletes and the greatest thought leaders of all time have used the power of visualisation to make their goals a reality and you can too!

Enhancements

Enhance your intentions and manifest them faster by writing or speaking them into existence. A different part of your brain is fired when you do this. Don't just think, write them down, and affirm them daily!

Freedom

Install new habits. Your brain installs new habits via three learning pathways. Emotion, Association and Repetition. You can become truly free of any limiting beliefs that are holding you back by following the steps above on a daily basis. To speed up your progress, you could book a session with a reputable Hypnotherapist.

It is absolutely worth striving to be the best version of yourself. Living a limited life is painful – spiritually, emotionally and then physically. If you feel any kind of physical pain in your body at all, listen to it and don't wait forty years like I did.

It's time to become your own Michelangelo. Chip away to reveal the beauty and magnificence within and your life will look very different just twelve months from now.

Be authentically you. You are not your labels, but you can own your identity. Now is your time to shine!

About Dee Twentyman

Dee is a trainer and consultant in Hypnotherapy and Psychotherapy, specialising in the treatment of chronic pain. She is also the author of *Subconscious Medicine - Understanding the Mind and Body Connection to Pain*, showing how to use the immense power of your mind to bring harmony and balance into your life.

Drawing on her years of personal experience suffering with IBS and migraines, she navigated her way from *suffering* to a life free of symptoms using what has now become her proven *Embarrassment to Empowerment System.* She now mentors thousands of people every year to transform their lives by giving them tools and strategies they can use for life.

Dee works predominantly with the emotional and psychological components of physical pain and has a private practice in Newcastle upon Tyne, England. She offers online consultations globally, as well as personal development courses and wellness programs in the corporate and education sectors.

Contact Dee Twentyman

dee@resonanceholisticsltd.com

www.resonanceholisticsltd.com

www.facebook.com/resonanceholistics

www.instagram.com/resonanceholistics

How To Use The Power Of S.E.L.F.L.O.V.E. To Catapult Your Movement

Lisa King The Self-Loveologist

"Self-love is the ultimate gift you can give yourself and those around you. With self-love, everything is possible."

Did you know that self-love is the ultimate gift you can give yourself and everyone else around you? The way you show up for yourself, the way you value yourself and your life not only creates your best life, it also shows others how to treat you.

Self-love is about creating a life where you have internal validation, where external factors are not needed for you to feel complete, and you do not need to be around others to feel whole. When you practice self-love consistently you will experience the inner peace and joy you deserve. This attracts the right people to you and repels the wrong people away from you too, catapulting your movement forward in the direction you want, with the people you want.

It is crucial to all of us that we make self-love a priority, but why is now the perfect time for you to make it happen? Why wait! Why continue along a path that you are not completely happy with when you can have everything you have ever wanted for yourself and more. Raising your vibration to be completely aligned both personally and professionally will bring you the kind of joy and happiness that lights you up. You show others what is possible and that they too can feel the joy for life that you feel.

Now is the time to take action, one step at a time. Now is the moment to create the life you want on YOUR terms, to fulfil your brilliance, and enjoy the life you truly deserve to have.

How do I know what a difference self-love makes, you may be asking? I've been on my own journey and I now live the life I have always wanted. However, it wasn't always like that. Not at all.

Growing up I had no self-respect or self-worth. You would never have known it though, as the masks and coping mechanisms were so well rehearsed and fixed in place, no-one would've known what was really going on. A little five-year-old girl that heard, saw and felt every punch, every vile word and every form of abuse her mum suffered at the hands of her dad. Feeling ashamed, guilty, unsafe and unworthy of love led to so many negative beliefs and coping mechanisms. Little would she know that her life was like a snowball rolling downhill, picking up more and more evidence of these negative beliefs, growing bigger and bigger as the years went by. Until one day, that snowball came crashing down, smashing everything into tiny pieces. That was the day her life changed forever.

Up until this point you would have seen a 38-year-old successful businesswoman, lots of friends, money to spend, great social life, property owner… life was great, or so it seemed!

Until that cold winter's day in January, 2010. Becky, my partner, and best friend, took her own life. One of the most beautiful and courageous women I knew was gone. To say I was completely shattered was an understatement.

A year of self-destructing followed, going back to my old coping mechanisms of drinking, drugs, casual sex, excessive working hours and playing hard. Only now, it was taking its toll on my body in so many ways. If I couldn't take stock of my life now after losing Becky, it would be my funeral next.

My breakdown wasn't really a surprise. I'm amazed my body held up as long as it did with the amount of abuse it suffered over the years. I was at my lowest point and knew something had to change. It had reached the point where the pain of change was less than the pain of staying the same. I had to become my priority. It was time to reconnect with the real Lisa, using the skills I had harnessed throughout my life. It was time to use my strength, drive, tenacity, and more, to create my new life. A life surrounded by the right people to inspire, drive and support me along the way.

Today, my outer world may not appear to have changed to those looking in. It is my inner world that has changed significantly.

The strategies I put in place over the last 30 years to reach this point had worked, but there was a cost. I was exhausted, unfulfilled, unhappy and I knew my life needed to change. I'd had enough. My body was clearly keeping score, physically breaking down, time and time again, yet I carried on and ignored it way too long.

My advice to you: don't wait for a tragedy to make the changes you know you need to make. Why fall further, making the journey longer, when you can make the change you need to make now. I had to look at what was impacting me the most. Awareness, recognition and action were needed to create the change I wanted and needed to see. Perhaps you are at that stage in your life now too? If so, here are some of the success principles I followed on my S.E.L.F.L.O.V.E. journey that you can follow too:

Stress

Stress comes in many different forms: physical, emotional, spiritual, financial and mental to name a few. It can also show itself in many ways, such as illness, negative emotions, reactions... there are many.

Look at what particular things are creating stress in your life right now?

Which things can you change, stop or reduce?

Asking yourself empowering questions to find a solution, rather than focusing on the problem, is a powerful tool to use. Questions delivering empowering answers, like *How can I....* rather than *Why is this....* are a great place to start.

Environment

Your environment plays a huge role in your wellbeing - people and places especially. So it is key to keep your environment clear of as much negative energy as possible.

Who no longer enhances your life?

Do you need to declutter your life?

You need to prioritise you and your needs from this moment on if you really want to serve and support others to the best of your ability.

Language

Your inner self talk is one of the most powerful ways you can create negativity or the very same tool can be used to create positivity in your life. For example, *I'm not good enough*, can be changed to *I'm doing my very best right now*, or *I am enough right now.* Recognising when you are using negative language is a great first step, then changing that language to a positive affirmation will result in huge steps forward.

Focus

When you focus on the present moment, you cannot be in the past or the future. The past is where depression can live, and the future is where you might find yourself anxiously worrying about what could happen. A good tip to stay present is to use your senses. Focus on where you are in that moment and look around you.

What can you see? Describe it.

Then focus on what you can hear. What does it sound like?

Then touch it. How does it feel?

You can also do this when you are eating. What are you eating? What does it taste like?

Lessons

I kept experiencing patterns of either negative behaviour or recurring things happening that I didn't want. Initially, I hadn't noticed them until I looked deeper. I believe these patterns are happening to show us something, to teach us. So when something happens that may be creating negative emotions for you, look at what it is trying to show you and ask it what it is trying to teach you.

What do you need to look at, address or change to ensure this pattern is interrupted or stopped?

Opportunities

If a great opportunity comes your way, say yes and work out the how afterwards. How many times have you wished you had not let that amazing opportunity pass you by? Your mind will want to keep you safe with your old patterns of thinking. The key is say yes before you talk yourself out of it!

Vulnerability

Do you see vulnerability as a weakness or a superpower? It can feel so uncomfortable asking for help when you have no control over the outcome. Taking yourself out of your comfortable zone on a daily basis, no matter how big or small, will strengthen your vulnerability muscle. Give it a go and make vulnerability your superpower.

Expectations

You will never be able to satisfy everyone, and you will never please everyone. Other's expectations of you are not your expectations. Being true to you and creating your own truth and expectations are key.

Understanding that my life experiences, although traumatic and hugely impactful, actually taught me so many crucial life-changing skills that turned out to be amazing. I just needed to recognise these and harness them in the right direction. With the right support, I became unstoppable.

Now it's time for you to become unstoppable by following the S.E.L.F.L.O.V.E. principles above! It's time to become your amazing, unique self and be unapologetically you, Perfekly Imperfect, exactly as you are!

About Lisa King

Lisa King is an international best-selling author and TEDx speaker. She is a multi-passionate entrepreneur, self-loveologist and mentor who gifts others the ability to realise theirs, by igniting their own beliefs of self-love.

Her fun love-for-life attitude, combined with her unstoppable leadership, drive and passion to help others, has seen Lisa create multiple businesses and brands that have created a huge ripple effect for so many.

In the last three years Lisa has focused on creating her own bespoke personal development events, workshops, online courses, online membership, and in the last year was the lead author and the driving force behind the Stories of Truth and Triumph book series with all profits going to Megan's Space Charity.

Lisa has launched many brands including trademarking Perfekly Imperfect™. This brand has multiple products all about showing up as your unique self and being unapologetically you - Perfekly Imperfect™.

Contact Lisa King

lisa@clarityfocusandgrowth.com

Facebook: https://www.facebook.com/lisaking49

Instagram: @1isaking

LinkedIn: Lisa King

TEDx Talk: https://www.youtube.com/watch?v=t87cz2Lii7A

A Synthesis Of Soul Wisdom Nine Steps To Owning Your Identity Through Soul Wisdom

Lorna M Munro - The Shamanic Synthesist

"Freedom is an inner revolution when you embrace where you are, right here, right now."

The Serenity Prayer talks of the wisdom to know the difference.

It was a long road for me to get to know what this meant. Wisdom is far more than intellect and I really wanted to know who I was.

To get a deeper knowing of my Soul was quite the journey. Intellectual knowing limited me to play small from the inside, yet to the outside world I was this BIG Scottish lassie, intimidating to some and very confident to others. Yet I struggled with choices. I struggled with my emotions and I struggled with life. I didn't know how to own who I was and struggled with how to show up in the world. Many do not know this about me. I'm letting you into my secrets now!

I was an only child until the age of twelve when my sister was born, followed by my youngest sister a few years later. As an only child I didn't think it unusual to talk to my friends from another realm. But at four years old I was told I was too old for imaginary friends and that was that. It was just me and my over-active imagination from then on.

I became deaf to my inner space where my greatest authority lived. I started to listen to the giants on the external planes.

My mind felt hijacked by an education system that I had a love hate relationship with, leading my adolescent inner rebel to stick two fingers up and walk away. I'd had enough! Little did I know then that it would take me down a road of serious suicidal thoughts. I had many of them, momentarily not wanting to be here, but I had deep sense of knowing suicide was not on the agenda.

I was emotionally crippled and looked for another human to hold me up, which I managed with great ease. I married too young for all the wrong reasons and jumped straight from the frying pan into the fire. My marriage had been verbally and mentally abusive for years, but now I was to experience physical abuse too. I played my part in all of this. There is no one to blame, but oh boy I could point my finger, blame and complain back then. If only he would stop drinking... blah, blah, blah...

After an Near Death Experience (NDE) rendered me a cripple with a fractured skull, I'd already been on the road to hell, but now I was at the gates ready to fall in! Cocktails of anti-depressants were my daily menu, along with alcohol and other substances. This was when I was met with the reality of how to commit suicide. Thank goodness it didn't happen, or I wouldn't be writing this now.

I was told I was a lost Soul, but I wanted to know how to find myself again. I realised I'd not known myself from the day I was born. I didn't know who I was and had no real identity. I'd been conditioned by everything and everyone external to me. Have you ever felt this way? Have you ever felt like you've become someone else for everyone else? I realised I had to change my mindset if I was going to open myself up to new possibilities. This was a game-changer.

The wrong people in my life started to leave and new people came in.

I then had what is called an Out of Body Experience (OBE). I was so intrigued that I went back to college and re-trained. I felt like I'd been given a new lease of life with a blank slate to have another go at it. I started practicing daily gratitude for this amazing new life that started to build around me.

Are you practicing gratitude daily?

By living in the energy of gratitude every day I saw how all the pieces of me, the grand synthesis of mind, body and spirit came to be. I saw how improving my mindset led to awakening my body by really listening to it. I connected with my soul on my body's terms, not my mind. Pain started to dissolve and knowing emerged from within me. I discovered this journey of transformation and developed a new system called Synthesis for your Soul that I now teach my clients as I build my Global Synthesis Movement.

What I learned most is we are all uniquely and imperfectly perfect. Yes, you are too! You and I are part of an intricate tapestry called life. We are one Soul interconnected to a cosmic sea of creation where only love reigns. You are part of this great co-creation; this Synthesis of Life and your commitment to your Soul's urge is what's calling you to step up now and own your identity.

Are you listening to the calling of your Soul? If you are ready to go to the next level, let's walk through a lite version of the S.Y.N.T.H.E.S.I.S. System now and take positive steps in the right direction. Grab your pen and paper, let's go!

Soul

Create a bridge to your Soul by hearing what it's saying to you. Get quiet and use a voice recorder to say what your soul wants you to know. Listen back to it. What's your soul telling you? Making this a daily practice will enable you to stay tuned into your higher power.

Your Inner Genius

Identify the sweet spot of your inner genius by taking four different colouring pens or pencils. Draw a mandala (circle) on a blank sheet of paper or use your journal. Close your eyes and ask your Soul the question, *Who am I?* Draw whatever comes into your mind, intuitively choosing the colours that feel right. Your Soul will show you the WAY *(Who Are You?)*. When you feel complete in that session, look at what your soul revealed to you. Some days it may not make sense! Other days it will be completely clear. Making this creative process part of your daily practice will give your mind and soul the ability to communicate faster with each other.

Nourishment

Recognise when you are self-sabotaging and catch it quickly by changing your inner dialogue. Write out three positive intention statements now and stick them where you'll continuously be reminded to affirm them. Use statements that will help you feel in control, such as *I accept myself as enough; I am living my best life*; or *I am leading by example*. Now write your own and feel them, absorbing them into your body.

Transformation

Take time out to reflect on your transformation so far. This will help you build trust in yourself. Journal one thing over the next few days that has successfully changed already in your business and/or life. These will become three great inner resources to tap into when you feel in a low mood and need to shift your mindset.

Humility

Practice daily gratitude. Being grateful for what you already have perfectly highlights your ability to call great things into your life. If there are other things you want to call into your life, get grateful for them already being on their way and feel what it's like to already have them in your life. Notice how your body reacts when you write them out. What reactions do you notice?

Elevation

Keep your vibration high and you'll witness your life changing. Living your life in a high vibrational way enables you to see and feel all the new potentials and possibilities making their way into your life. Take your coloured pens/pencils and draw something that will make your soul soar. Feel the joy rising and let your inner child out to play!

Surrender

Recognise any old thought patterns causing you to limit your life. When you limit your life, you limit your business. Dissolve any limiting behaviours and them to let go. I recommend dancing it out! Search for *Five Rhythms* on YouTube and let yourself go.

Integrity

With honest daily appraisals you'll become in-tune and aware of your mind, body and spirit's interconnectedness. Be rigorously honest about how YOU are showing up in the world each day. Who are you being when you are at your best? Who are you being when you are at your worst? Keep journaling your journey.

Synchronicity

Own your identity by learning your Soul's own song. If you had a song, what would it be? Anchoring this song is a powerful way to remember who you are and why you are here. Journal your song into existence and sing it to yourself when you need to get back into your highest vibration.

Welcome to the grand synthesis of radical self-acceptance by recognising your Soul's true song and now see your magnificence shining in this new world created by YOU. It's your time to explore the limitless possibilities that await you. Enjoy!

About Lorna Munro

Lorna is an international best-selling author, speaker, Shamanic practitioner, holistic health therapist, spiritual coach, intuitive visionary and transformational fire-walking instructor. She also holds a Cosca Counsellor Skills Certification.

After a *Near Death Experience (NDE),* Lorna embarked on healing herself from past mental, emotional, physical and spiritual abuse which she had hidden deep within her psyche.

An *Out of Body Experience (OBE)* many years later led her into training with other healing modalities, latterly moving into frequency/vibration medicine. Lorna owns a Holistic Health Practice in the Scottish Highlands where she runs workshops and various online programmes.

Presently, Lorna is using a medically certified frequency device and is training as a guide with the Transformational Certified System of the Gene Keys to assist visionaries, like you, in your holistic wellbeing journey.

Contact Lorna Munro

www.holistichealthinverness.co.uk

Instagram.com/lorna_m_munro

www.lornamunro.weebly.com

https://genekeys.com/ref/1239

The Call Of Freedom

Penny Layzell - The Freedom ReActivator

"With freedom comes choice, with choice comes the power to truly be."

Who am I to talk of freedom? Me who has spent most of her life shackled to the system. A regime that most of us live by. The get up, do as you are told, be on time regime. The Oh yes you have had a hard life but hasn't everyone regime.

My life has been fully about this regime. For so many years I struggled under the weight of the regime much like the majority of the population. I have suffered crippling anxiety, agoraphobia, depression, and like most I have soldiered on pulling myself together to get on, show up and hide away at the end of the day.

How did I get to this point? The point where fear became my go to and my mind allowed this to control me? When had I become a robot going through the motions of putting everyone first in a bid to show the world that I was successful?

I know the day it started.

I was just five years old when mum grabbed me by the throat and pinned me to the bed. This incident sparked so much fear in me, my default became protect myself at all costs. It was the start of a tremendously turbulent relationship between us. I resented my sister and the love mum showered on her due her learning disabilities.

From an early age I could feel energy strongly. I would connect with guides and this difference didn't help me fit in with society, so I withdrew inwards. When dad was away, I learned that the safest place was on my own, locked in my own thoughts and my own loneliness.

When I was nine my parents made the decision to leave military life behind and relocate. I faced another challenge. The challenge of fitting in… again. Here were children who had grown up together. I was weirdly quiet and withdrawn and had a bizarre accent from living all over the place. At this point I was really struggling with home life. Dad worked a lot, my sister and I fought all the time, and mum and I barely spoke. I was also facing bullying and isolation at school.

Dad, who was so immensely proud of me, wanting me to have only the best, took to planning out my future. I took to drinking and was sneaking into the local bars by 14. I was so low and depressed; I can't tell you how many times I contemplated suicide. Some nights I could be found curled up in a ball with the knife at my wrists, just willing myself to have the courage to do it. Even at that I failed.

My shyness and awkwardness were so profound I couldn't speak to anyone. I learned to hide the real me and become what everyone wanted me to be. I fitted in by slipping under the radar.

By 19, I was pregnant and faced being a single working mum, but my daughter was my salvation. I finally had something and someone to live for. Someone who made me want to be the best person I could possibly be. I wanted to be the best mum for her. I wanted to show her it was possible to live a fulfilled life. I learned the lesson that in giving her all I could, I could feel truly fulfilled.

I met my husband at 21 and married at 23, and after losing a couple of babies, we finally completed our family with two additional daughters. We were alone with no family support for much of the time, juggling family life and work so much that we became experts at hardly seeing each other. We made it work with pure grit and determination. Again, the lesson was: look after everyone and fulfilment would follow.

Mum became sick with breast cancer at the beginning of 2015, my default setting of put everyone before me and I would be fine kicked in. That was until mum passed away on 21 December and I received my own breast cancer diagnosis on the 23rd.

Again, my default setting kicked in protect everyone and I will be OK. I threw myself into work and getting through my cancer treatment. I negotiated my treatment and chose the quickest surgeries so I could continue working throughout. In fact, I didn't have one day off sick. I used my annual leave for any days I needed to ensure we didn't have a loss of income and I carried on. Some days I could barely get out of bed, yet I carried on.

In the process, I shut out the one person who loved me with all his heart, my husband. I couldn't cope with him fussing and I was determined that I could hold everything together.

By the middle of 2016, my marriage was seriously struggling, and my life was falling apart again. Determined to hold it together I continued to put myself last and fought to keep everyone else going. I had become a prisoner to my default setting.

By the beginning of 2017, something clicked in me and I began a journey of self-discovery. I finally started to understand life and in late 2019, I felt the call of my Higher Self. The call was so strong that it made me stop and delve deeper into me. I learned who I was, who I truly was, and what I found astounded me. I came to understand my journey, the fear within that had so impacted my life and the way I was.

I now take my clients through a journey from fear to success and have documented some of the practices I use at work in my book The Power of Freedom in the Corporate World. My biggest advice to you is to understand your fears and what is holding you back.

One of the processes I teach my clients at the very start of their journey is the following activity, as it was only in understanding my identity that I was able to move forward, which in turn created my success.

I would love you to set aside some time to identify where you are now and whether anything needs to change. Set the intention to work on yourself over the next five working days.

Days 1 and 2

When that alarm goes off, notice your reaction.

a) Do you reach immediately for the snooze button?

b) Do you turn off the alarm, but not move immediately?

c) Do you jump straight out of bed?

Note down which one you answered yes to.

Days 3 and 4

Set your alarm 30 minutes before you are due to get up and ensure you have a notebook and pen by your bed. Once the alarm goes off don't move from the bed. Pick up your notebook and just allow your feelings to flow. Write the first thoughts that come into your mind. Do not read through it or judge it, just write.

Day 5

Day 5 is the day for analysation, and I recommend you do this at the end of the day when you have time to work through your feelings.

Did you discover that you are you jumping straight out of bed on days one and two? If so, it is likely you are in a good place regarding your work. If not, then something may be out, and you can do some work around this in a moment.

Now take time to read through your morning thoughts from

days three and four. Take all this information in sitting quietly and feel into how you are feeling now. What areas are highlighted for change for you?

This is such a useful exercise to centre and rebalance you, and to gain an understanding of any fear holding you back. I would love you to keep journaling in this fashion too, just letting the thoughts flow.

My clients find just taking this initial step enables them to start addressing their fears, and it helps them to identify who they are and what is holding them back. Although there is a fuller process of working through this fear (and in doing so it positively impacts your work success, and balances your home life), this initial step will enable you to have an insight into who you are now and who you can be.

I can only imagine if we all owned our identity and worked *free* in this way, how much we could change the world.

About Penelope Layzell

Penelope spent over 30 years within the corporate world feeling tied to the constraints of her 9-5 job, but at the same time loving the power and career she had forged for herself.

During her time, she learned to hide; hide who she was and who she was born to be. Fitting in with the expectations of what was expected in order to succeed. In doing so, she suffered the loss of her health, loss of balance and loss of who she was. Upon discovering herself again, she learned to listen intuitively to herself, and in doing so found even more success flowed.

She now supports others to find their inner voice, working differently to the expected way, helping them to create balance and harmony throughout their own lives in both work and at home.

Contact Penelope Lyzell

penelope@diamension.co.uk

www.diamension.co.uk

www.facebook.com/diamensionbusiness

Part Two

Own Your VALUE

Stop Making Excuses And Make Your D.R.E.A.M. A Reality For Every Dream You Give Up On, There Are A Thousand More Ways You Could Have Tried

Jenni Winter-Leach - The Equestrian Mindset Mentor

"Why Waste Energy Wishing, When You Can Use It Building Your Dream?"

I look up at him. He is so beautiful. His face is soft and pure white, his eyes are a contrasting deep brown. Like deep dark water that can draw you in and hold you in its profound wisdom. Staring into them I am lost in a place that I want to stay forever.

"Jenni, leave him alone please" says my mother. 'We have to go now', as she holds out her hand to spirit me away.

I was just four years old. I had been drawn to the fence on a walk with my family. The same pull every time I came across one of these stunning, spirited animals - the horse.

A giant, beholding a huge head, a nose as soft as velvet and such curiosity in his eyes. It equalled the curiosity I had. What would it be like to sit on the back of such a beautiful creature, wrap my arms round his neck, bury my face into his soft hair? To have the feeling of flying through the air, my legs not touching the ground. What would it be like to have horses in my life?

My family had never been interested in horses. There was no

obvious reason why I felt I had to steal every possible chance I had to be around these incredible creatures. Yet finally on my seventh birthday, I sat on my parents' bed and opened their card. Tears filled my eyes. A riding lesson! My parents had actually bought me the one thing I had dreamt about every night of what felt like my whole life.

Over the following decade, at every possible opportunity I had, I was with horses. Having my own wasn't an option until I graduated university, but my passion never waned. I would cry at the thought of one day having horses as a fundamental part of my life. Having the chance to be around them whenever I desired and not just on the weekends.

At age 29, I reached a decision point on a hot Sunday evening that would change my future, forever. As I cleared away the happy mess from the classroom I had been training in all day, I found the same tears streaming down my face again.

"Why are you crying, Jenni?" said a wise lady named Elaine. She had just experienced the transformational two days of equine-assisted coaching that I had delivered that weekend.

"I don't want to get back on a plane tomorrow and fly to another country to do the job that takes me away from everything I love. I want to be doing this!"

"So, what's is stopping you?"

"Money is stopping me. How can I leave my highly paid corporate career to do this? I know there is no money in horses. My whole family always told me so. I need another two years to even consider having made enough money to leave my job and make this happen. I'm just about managing to keep my one horse now. How on earth can I still keep her and change my career at the same time?"

"Do you know how many years you've been saying that, Jenni?" Elaine paused. "Two years. How many more will it take before you make the decision and follow your dream?"

In that exact moment I realised. Time wasn't the enemy. Money wasn't the issue. Fear was. My belief that *there was no money in horses* held me back from creating the life I had dreamt of since I was a child. The life that still bought me to tears when I considered the possibility. I knew without a doubt that was the life I really wanted. I had to make a decision. I had to make a plan. I had to try!

Have you ever put important things off?

Why do we put so many things off and let go of what we truly dream we can be, have, or do? It's like life is something guaranteed, or time is something we will always have.

Maybe it can wait until we have more money, experience or support? Sadly, time is the one thing that is outside of our control. Time isn't that luxury we think it is. Decisions are. Our decisions drive everything in life. Any change starts with just one thing. A decision.

So, I wrote the most important email I've ever written in my life. The one that started, *Please accept my resignation...*

Of course, I didn't just leave my job and my dream life appeared. I made a plan and worked out, at best, the first part of it. I had no real idea how I would make a career out of it. I did at least know how to generate a bit of income, things I could change, give up and do differently to start making other things a possibility. I also knew that having the right support around me was going to be vital to my success.

My head and heart were full of many fears. *What if... I couldn't pay my bills, I couldn't get clients, I wasn't as good as the others, I wasn't experienced enough...* The list went on.

Every time I faced one of my fears, I had to own it. I had to go inwards and ask myself:

What if you can?

What if you are?

What do you really want?

Each time I answered one of those question I would then ask:

What is the outcome if you don't try?

What is one thing you can do to make this happen?

What is one step you can take to give it a go?

Slowly and steadily but surely the plan came together. People were actually willing to part with their money to have me support them. They were inspired by what I had done. It was terrifying and exhilarating all at the same time!

I was spending my time at the stables with people and their horses, and I had quality time with my own horse too. I had somehow created a way to *make money from horses* and it didn't involve mucking out stables, standing outside in the pouring rain or spending long hours doing back breaking work. The very thing that I had grown up thinking was completely impossible, I had made happen.

Eight years on from that resignation letter and I have the life I dreamt of. I have the freedom to be with my beautiful horse Sirius, who is actually a big white horse with huge brown eyes! I get to help others to overcome their fears and reach their dreams. I am the one speaking on the stages, networking and enjoying my time at equine events, which I used to save every bit of holiday time to enjoy.

I absolutely love what I do.

Horses are an everyday part of my life and to top it all off, I earn far more than I did in my corporate role. I now have new dreams and I fully intend to make those happen.

How did I make it happen and how can you do it too? I kept following a process in my head. It took five simple steps and kept on repeating them. Simply D.R.E.A.M.

1. Decide

Is this a dream *you* would actually love to make a reality? Or just something other people have talked about or done? Is it something you can influence the outcome of? What decision do you need to make today so that you can live your dream life?

2. Realise

Define exactly what this destination will be like. Travel forward into your future, make it a reality in your head. Imagine it has already happened. Does it have the essence of something without being exact? Make it real. Gain every bit of information that you can.

3. Engineer

Work backwards from step 2. Knowing it has already happened, what was the step you took right before you achieved the dream? What was the one before that? The one before that? Come all the way back to tomorrow (or later today). Think about the *first few steps* you took to at least get on the path towards your desires. A journey of a thousand miles starts with just one step.

4. Acknowledge

Face any fears and acknowledge them. *Own them.* Explore them. Fear exists in the future. It hasn't actually happened. The steps above have shown you how resourceful you can be. By working backwards, you already overcame potential obstacles in the plan. You can do it.

5. Move

Imagine taking the *first* step. Then the next few. Notice how it feels. What is it like to know you are making a conscious effort to making your dream a reality? Now do it.

When you look back in ten years' time, what will you still be wishing had happened? What is the cost of not taking any action and staying just the same?

Are you going to take your dream to the grave? In your last hours what will you wish you had been brave enough to try?

Change your future.

Make that decision today.

Follow your D.R.E.A.M. and make it happen.

About Jenni Winter-Leach

Jenni Winter-Leach is an award-winning international speaker, best-selling author, in-demand trainer and Equestrian Mindset and Performance Psychology Master Coach. She is also the Founder of the Equestrian Development and Empowerment Network - a global movement supporting horse riders to perform at their best and enjoy their passion.

Growing up hearing *there is no money in horses*, Jenni spent her early career accelerating fast in global talent management consultancy for a world-leading telecoms company. She quickly realised that her passion and talents were supporting people to be their best. Her entrepreneurial mindset, ability to solve problems and passion for competing horses led her to set up Flying Changes Mindset. In the last few years, she steered her company from an idea to a six-figure global business, quickly accelerating Jenni as one of the UK's leading Equestrian Mindset and Performance Experts.

Jenni turned her childhood dream into a reality – now you can do it too!

Contact Jenni Winter-Leach

www.contactjenni.me

How To Make It Without Faking It

Grant Murrell - The Success Pilot

"Life is an opportunity that's too good not do something wonderful with it!"

Have you ever heard of the phrase, fake it until you make it? How does it make you feel? Maybe you squirm in your seat. Perhaps it empowers you to make your next bold move with courage. Whatever reaction you have, let's talk about how you can make it without faking it. Let's dig deeper together to explore how you can build your integrity-driven movement by really owning your value.

I'm super passionate about this topic because it is one of the underlying factors behind success. Success has always been a fascination, an obsession in fact, since I was just 14 years of age. What actually is success anyway? It can be defined in so many ways; financial, physical, emotional, mental, spiritual, relational, and charitable, to name a few. However, in my experience, regardless of the area you choose to measure, it's all built on a few key factors:

Having confidence

Believing in yourself

Being it

Owning that space

Sounds daunting? It doesn't have to be, I promise you.

There's another reason I chose to write this subject and it's because I know that approaching things in the wrong order can be very costly in terms of time, money and energy.

Using this philosophy first can save you a fortune on marketing costs, thousands of hours (time being your most valuable asset), and a headful of stress and frustration.

In this complicated world, many things compete for your focus and resources, so I'll make your success strategy simple, yet effective and empowering. I encourage you to grasp, embody and start acting on this today! But before you do, join me on a little journey back in time for a moment so you can learn a big lesson quickly.

It's a Friday in July 1992 and as I lay back on the floor of my Volkswagen camper van and look skywards, I can see small clouds high in the sky as the sun beats down. The radio plays softly as I drift in and out of a beautiful hazy sleep. It's the kind of sleep that's so easy to experience on such a beautiful day as this.

As my mind drifts, I imagine a music video; one that could work perfectly with the song that's playing softly on the radio. I remember the video distinctly; a hot summer's day looking up at a church bell tower in a hot, dry climate. As the bell swings, it chimes, punctuating the song perfectly like a hedonistic chant.

Suddenly, I am crudely halted by the sound of an agitated voice, "Where's Grant? Where the hell is he?" It's Phil, the site foreman.

In my early years, I played in a band that very nearly made the grade, and as many musicians will tell you, you'd undertake an array of part-time jobs to pay for guitar strings, or to buy fuel for your next gig. Well, this construction site was one such example and Phil was the ferocious site foreman - a real taskmaster always on the war path. Phil stands outside the iconic old van, bewildered where I am.

I squeeze myself lower down on the floor of the van so he doesn't see me having an 'extended lunch break'.

Now please think kindly of me as I actually worked quite hard and trust me when I tell you that I'd never do that now. However, that became a pivotal day in my life towards the businesses I run today. You see, Phil was known for springing on people and asking them three key questions:

- *What have you been doing?*
- *Where are you going?*
- *What are you doing next?*

He knew within seconds if you'd been skiving by the way you answered his questions.

Like most others, I either shuffled uncomfortably or gave an unconvincing answer before he'd bellow, "You're making it up, show me what you've been doing."

After being caught out twice, I decided skiving was really hard work and quite stressful. I became increasingly curious about just how hard it would be to simply do what I'd been pretending to do. To my surprise, the tasks asked weren't that hard and when doing them life became less stressful. I even gained a feeling of accomplishment and confidence from having done them.

When Phil next asked his three magic questions, I could answer them without a second thought. In fact, he only ever asked twice after that, when he'd simply look at me and say, "I don't need to ask you. I know you're getting things done, I can see it in your eyes."

So, there it was. All those years ago, I'd made that self-discovery in the most unlikely of circumstances. I didn't know it then, but this lesson was to play a much bigger role for me and hundreds of other business owners I would mentor across the globe.

Today, I see many people crouching behind their own metaphoric van doors and maybe you are doing it a little, or even a lot, too. Maybe you have found yourself making excuses that are costing time, money and energy. Perhaps you have created diversions or dilemmas that get between you and your passion, purpose and freedom. One thing's for sure, if you want to stop spinning your wheels and start creating your legacy, this chapter is your opportunity to change.

I often hear people self-defeating and creating obstacles that simply don't exist. Many talk to themselves in opinions or their truths, but not in facts.

What if you thought only in facts? Would your beliefs, actions and therefore your results change? Very possibly!

If you don't believe in yourself, or if you suffer from imposter syndrome, let me ask you this:

- *Could you honestly prove you're not good enough if I were to put you in front of a court of law?*
- *Could you really provide hard evidence that you aren't good enough to achieve what you really desire?*

The point is this: you imagine a great number of things about yourself that are not factually correct. If you were to believe in yourself based on facts, you wouldn't have to ask, *Grant, can I fake it until I make it?* By the way, my answer is always, *For a short time, maybe.* But before long, your version of Phil, the site foreman will appear and call you out, playing havoc with your self-esteem.

Let's change it to *shape it while you make it* instead. That's right, because all success is first created in your mind before it takes tangible form.

What would happen if you made a mental commitment to yourself that you will become the person you need to be, to achieve what you want to achieve?

What if you listed in priority order all the things you need to do to achieve your dreams and your ultimate goals?

Let's do it together now:

- *What are your most important dreams and goals?*
- *Who would you need to be to achieve them with ease and flow?*
- *What would you need to do consistently to ensure*
- *you are always making progress towards them?*
- *What could get in the way of you achieving these goals?*
- *Who would you need to call in for help to overcome those challenges?*

Getting clear on your answers to these questions will take you a great way towards making it without faking it. Most obstacles will get out your way when you decide to become the person you need to become, to do what you need to do, to achieve what you want to achieve in the way that you want to achieve it.

Success can be decided in just one moment, so make your success simple.

When you know what you want and you value yourself, you will become magnetic. You will begin to look different, feel different and obstacles will move out of your way. However, to really own your value, make sure to only talk to yourself in facts. Then, and only then, can you take actions with conviction and do what you need to do to achieve what you want to achieve. Let's look at some immediate facts that I already know about you:

You are brilliantly and uniquely you. You have life experience that nobody else on the planet has experienced the same way as you. You are closer than you think to realising your soul's purpose and potential. You are only ever just a few decisions away from building the business and life you desire.

Now is the time to up-level your commitment, up-level yourself and up-level your value. The world is waiting for you, so let's not keep it waiting any longer.

About Grant Murrell

Grant Murrell is fast becoming one of the most sought-after thought leaders in the arena of world class human communication. He is an international speaker, transformation expert, certified trainer in NLP and hypnotherapy, author, radio show presenter and entrepreneur.

Over the past 19 years, Grant and his international team have coached thousands of entrepreneurs and business leaders across 15 countries to increase profits by up to 200% often in just a few months. Working on their team, systems, mindset and strategy, they generate more money in less time with less stress, enjoying more fun and fulfilment in their life and business.

Grant's ultimate mission is to empower people to embrace their passion, purpose, freedom, wealth and happiness by designing their life, business, organisation or foundation to create a legacy.

Contact Grant Murrell

www.GrantMurrell.com

www.SuccessIsAFormula.com

www.instagram.com/grant.murrell

Get Over Yourself And Lead
Five Strategies For Transcending Your Fear Based Ego

Mary Gregory - The Conscious Leader's Coach

"The antidote to fear is love. So, practice self-compassion, recognise your strengths, own your value and create possibility from love."

How do you hold yourself back? Maybe an inner critic paralyses you, saying what you have to offer is uninteresting. Or maybe you start with good intention to focus on your marketing, only to realise the day has disappeared as other activities unconnected to your goals distracted you. You may have well-honed excuses for listening to your critic or helping the neighbour with their burst pipe or lost cat. Whether you like the idea or not, what's really getting in the way is fear. This activates your ego into unhelpful reactions and behaviours that stop you shining a light on your strengths and talents.

Your ego is a highly developed psychological defence system designed to keep you in your comfort zone. At the first sign of threat, your fear brings down shutters in the form of reactive behaviours that keep you safe. But here's the curious thing. When it comes to the laws of attraction, you are already attracting whether you are fearful or not. People, opportunities, things are moving towards you, and how you respond to these will be impacted by the extent you are driven by your fear-activated ego.

Take a look around you.

- How delighted and excited are you by what you see?
- Are you feeling frustrated or disappointed?
- What elements of your business are really working, and which aren't?
- How is the way you are being around this impacting you?

Through fear, you can become victim to your circumstances, saying yes to any work, compromising your value, and values. On one level, you are meeting your needs to be busy and earn a decent income, but a misalignment with your values risks your well-being and sending out an unconscious message that attracts more of what you don't want.

Some years ago, sparked by a particularly challenging phase when I was on the floor with emotional and physical exhaustion, I got interested in the whole notion of attraction. What had been a flood of opportunities was now a trickle. I was anxious about making the most of these, which leaked through my interactions and how I was being. Desperation is highly unattractive.

I sat back and faced some hard truths. The first was accepting I was responsible. Much as I wanted to blame my circumstances and other people, I realised this was futile. The bottom line was, I needed to own what I had created. My ego had been acting out big time.

I held a limiting belief that while I was busy with work, I didn't have time for marketing. This was my ego talking, justifying myself and my lack of action. I was inauthentic. The absolute truth was, I didn't bother with marketing because I was frightened of putting myself out there.

My internal critic would pose confidence draining questions. Some would come from a fear of success: *How could I cope with the responsibility that being successful would bring?*

Others from a fear of rejection: *What makes you think anyone would be interested in what you have to offer Mary?*

The impact was, I played small. I'd look at other people's marketing with admiration whilst feeling unable to find the words to write a tweet, let alone an article or, God forbid, pick up the phone! And being a people-pleaser and rescuer, I'd get involved in other people's dramas to such a degree they distracted me from my own life and building my own business.

I was getting in my own way. I was initially shocked to realise this, but ultimately empowered to transform my approach. I chose a different path which resulted in my developing the Five Conscious Rs™ for transcending your fears.

1. Responsibility
2. Recognition
3. Resources
4. Routine
5. Reward

These underpin an approach that provides a sense of grounded-ness and personal power. All serve to shift how you relate to yourself and show up in the world, impacting what you attract.

1. Responsibility

Consciously being responsible requires you to act with courage and self-compassion, so you learn to befriend your fear and act despite it.

This moves you from victim to chooser, putting you at the source of what you create and the chance to align your integrity. For me, integrity is all about keeping our word to ourselves and to others. If I live my life in tune with my values and keep promises, then fear decreases and personal power increases. Life and work become more manageable. When being responsible, I set boundaries around my work, relationships, and self-care. All contribute to attracting more of what I want in my life, and less of what I don't. Ask yourself:

- How are you responsible for what is showing up in your life, both the things that are working and not working?
- What choices are you making? How are these helping or hindering you?
- What might you want to create differently going forward?

2. Recognition

Recognition is about raising consciousness. It applies on many levels, in responding to your fear and taking steps that help you get over yourself.

Naming your fear or behaviour

By finding the words to recognise what is going on, you make explicit something that would otherwise be implicit. The challenge with unspoken fears is that they have power over us. Language raises our awareness and understanding so we can explore options to do something about it. For example, you promised yourself that you would call three contacts, yet half an hour later you are still scrolling through Instagram. Noticing and acknowledging this brings it to your consciousness and thereby a choice to do something about it.

Recognising your values, strengths and purpose

- What is important to you about how you live your life and why?
- How clear are you of your strengths and how you play to them?
- How do these illustrate your purpose and contribution to the world?

These are big, important questions. Knowing your answers provides a frame of reference that guides you when making decisions, overcoming adversity and maintaining focus. For example, when made redundant, my purpose and values guided my response, enabling me to play to my strengths and ensuring the ending was good for all parties.

Recognising and appreciating what is working

Name this and be grateful. What you focus on grows, and the more you become conscious and thankful for the positive things, the more you can create from that place.

3. Resources

Think about an everyday task, such as driving your car. How is your driving's quality affected by how much sleep you had the night before? Your performance is affected by your level of personal resources and sleep.

Resources are our reserves that keep our energy and capability topped up. When they are depleted, we are vulnerable to under-performing and succumbing to our fear.

We keep our resources topped up by taking care of ourselves physically, emotionally, mentally and spiritually. The more topped up your energy resources, the easier it is to transcend your fear, feel good about yourself and value yourself.

This particularly applies to making sure your emotional needs are met. For example, *I'm terrified at the thought of a presentation I've been asked to do. My fear keeps increasing as I procrastinate.*

Ask yourself: *what is it you need that will reduce your anxiety?* What comes up perhaps is your need to feel supported, so you reach out to a friend. You can then address your needs and making sure you do so, plays a critical part in building your confidence.

4. Routine

We are creatures of habits. Some are healthier than others. The challenge is that we are unconscious of most of our practices. It is worth reviewing your daily routine and habits to pinpoint the ones that help, and those that don't. Then create a conscious routine where you commit to five positive habits a day that contribute to you managing your fear, looking after your well-being and progressing your business.

For example:

- Morning meditation
- Setting an intention for your day ahead
- Check activities against strategic goals
- Walk in the fresh air
- 15 minutes reflection at the end of each day

5. Reward

This is last on the list; however, it mustn't be neglected. The more you have a dialogue of success in your head, the less room for your inner critic or self-doubting ego. It's invaluable to celebrate and reward your achievements. For example, when I've written an article or spoken to those three contacts that I'd promised myself to call, I can celebrate by walking my gorgeous dogs. Not only is this a rewarding experience, but I get the double whammy of topping up my energy resources too.

Transcend your fears about putting yourself and your brand out there by building the Five Conscious Rs™ into your approach to your life and business. This will maximise the contribution you are making in the world and not only will you have more fun and fulfilment, but you will attract more opportunities that align with who you really are.

About Mary Gregory

Mary Gregory is a sought-after international leadership consultant, committed to empowering leaders to create workplaces where people thrive. A trusted coach to executives and business owners and author of the best-selling book *Ego – Get Over Yourself And Lead*, she's led change for organisations including First Choice Holidays, Ralph Lauren, Tesco and was lead board and executive coach at Penna PLC.

Integrating her career experience, which began as a therapist in child and family psychiatry, with developing leaders and leading change in blue-chip organisations, Mary utilises deep understanding of what makes humans and organisations tick to enable sustainable change.

As well as coaching thousands of leaders, Mary designs lively and interactive programmes which put the learner at the centre of the experience. Her clients describe her as a warm, compassionate, challenging and tenacious coach who supports them to achieve results through expanding their thinking and taking positive, courageous action.

Contact Mary Gregory

www.marygregory.com

mary@marygregory.com

Ego to Essence
The Rise of A Phoenix

Bolutiwi Aiyesimoju - The Essence Magnifier

"It's time to give wings to your being and liberate your essence from limitation."

Did you know there are millions of high-achieving women around the world who believe they need to suppress their true selves to succeed?

I will never forget watching one of the highest-ranking women in L'Oréal become a pale version of herself in the presence of a male colleague she was trying to impress. She wore a perfectly tailored three-piece grey pinstriped trouser suit, a crisp white shirt, and expensive dark brogues. The caricature of bullish bravado that she donned like ill-fitting armour was in jarring contrast to the insightful, confident and charismatic leader she was.

It struck me as odd that even at that stage in her career, she's needed to play to the gallery. The sad truth is that she felt the need to fit in. Distasteful as it was to watch, it was a valuable lesson. Somewhere deep inside of me a seed was planted, and I am now building a global movement to inspire over one million high achieving women to Magnify their essence for more conscious impact. It's time to own your *shine!*

Today we're experiencing a global shift and so many are questioning the status quo. Increasingly, employees and visionary business owners wish to express more of their whole selves at work and in business. The weaknesses in the old way of doing things are becoming glaringly apparent. The limitations of unbridled ego and its constructs, created to project images that protect have left us exposed and fragile in the face of the unknown. In other words, our immense ignorance is only dwarfed by our pride, prejudice and pretence. It has never been so important for us to liberate ourselves from the constraints of ego as we step into a new age. In the age of essence, we tune into our true power as we recognise and embrace the total possibilities of the present moment.

Speaking of possibilities, there is the story of how I manifested a job at the largest cosmetics company in the world without actually applying. For now, I'm going to share how excitement gave way to disillusionment on my fast-track to burnout.

After a year and a half in my first role working in Paris at L'Oréal, I was offered a role as Diversity and Ethics Manager for Industry, a brand-new role. This was my version of heaven. I took the time to observe, reflect, consult, and create. I focused mainly on diversity and learned as much about my own biases, based on stereotypes and prejudices, as those whom I interviewed. I realised that awareness was key to understanding unconscious biases which led to certain groups, including French, Caucasian women from the best schools, feeling they needed to repress parts of themselves to fit in.

My proposed solution was diversity and equity training for which I got the buy-in of several powerful leaders without whom it would not have been possible to get traction at the group level. I was asked to lead the group effort to roll it out in collaboration with the Global Training Department. For months, I patiently answered all the questions about the programme

I had created. I had thought I was amongst friends.

One day, I got an email that tore the programme apart. I immediately called my colleague from the training department to share the horrid news. No answer! Several phone calls and emails later, it dawned on me that I'd been played. Ever heard the expression, *Keep your friends close and your enemies closer?* He had accepted to work with me only to get as much information as he could out of me, so the training could be rolled out without me. This hit me like a ton of bricks. I felt a deep sadness that transcended feeling sorry for myself. I just could not understand how anyone could be so low. This was a painful first-hand experience of the pitfalls of ego-driven, territorial corporate politics. I felt totally betrayed.

The attacks become relentless, and something deep within me knew that I had to choose between email spars and success. If I wanted my goal of training all managers in my division in 12 months, I needed to keep my eye on the ball. My essence trumped over my ego's need to engage. All emails from antagonistic parties were delegated to my managers. Once they stepped in and stood up for me and the project, it was difficult for my persecutors to continue the witch-hunt, so aggressively.

It wasn't over though. I recall one meeting with the VP of Human Resources. On one side of the board table were two people from the Global Training Team and on the other side was a powerful leader and I. When the VP came in and asked what the status was with the diversity project, a long list of all the reasons why we could not start the training that year were shared by the training team. The VP acknowledged them, looked over at me and asked, "Bolutiwi when can you start?"

"Tomorrow."

"You have my blessing!" I was free to go full steam ahead.

The fantastic news is that 1,300 managers were trained in 13 months thanks to the cooperation of several Division Directors and their HR teams. It was excellent experience in leadership by influence for me.

I went on to successfully manage several other projects and got a lot of visibility.

This experience, though fulfilling because I felt that it had positive societal impact, also knocked my confidence in human nature, leading me to build a protective wall around my essence. The years I spent at L'Oréal thereafter were coloured by my hurt. I definitely subconsciously questioned my intrinsic worth, which I now know led me to overcompensate. If only I had the support that I now give high achieving women. If only I had someone to help me navigate my inner state in a manner that did not leave undetonated mines that would blow up later, instead of being consciously diffused in a safe setting.

The reality is that when I couldn't find the support that I needed for myself, I created it! I now deliver the signature E.S.S.E.N.C.E. System worldwide supporting high-achieving women to be more conscious, impactful leaders. Here's a little sneaky-peak that you can take away with you, right now.

Expand

Allow and embrace your emotions. Even negative emotions, when felt and processed, can be sources of wisdom. One tip that works very well with my clients is, *Dive deep in the emotion to get the pearl of wisdom and then come back up for air.* There is no point splashing about continuously in a puddle or suppressing the emotion. What you resist persists.

Soar

When they go low, you go high! Remember that eagles don't squabble with chickens. This is about choosing to focus your energy on your vision no matter what the distractions may be. Just ask yourself, *If I had time and energy for just one thing what would I choose?* There is no shame in getting champions who can fight your corner, especially when it means you can focus on winning gracefully.

Shine

It is possible to have a significant impact, enjoying a balanced, fulfilling and purposeful life when you follow all five steps of the S.H.I.N.E. Bright - Dazzle Without The Frazzle programme that you can see in the illustration below.

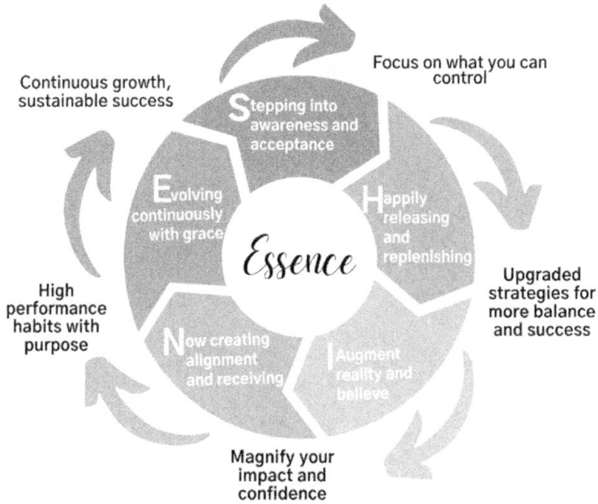

Embody Empowerment

Tune into the power of your magnificent essence. This is understanding that the power you seek is not outside of you. It is in you and lies in you being as authentic as possible. Be the power you seek!

Nurture

You can't give from an empty cup. The bigger the legacy the more you need to fill your cup by mental, emotional, physical and spiritual nurture. This is Self-Love 101. How are you currently filling up your cup?

Connect

To connect deeply with others, you need to connect with your essence. Working on self-awareness and acceptance are powerful steps towards enhanced self-love and consciousness. The more you love yourself, the more you can enjoy deep and meaningful relationships, which is exactly what Lisa King wrote about in her chapter on self-love at the beginning of this book!

Evolve

To truly be a leader, you must learn to be a genius and a student. Own it when you're brilliant and accept with grace and humility when you need to learn and grow. This way, you simply get better.

There are simply some things no one should have to do alone! Don't make the same mistake I made. Instead of listening to the warning signs of exhaustion, and seeking support and solutions proactively, I bottled up my pain and pretended I was fine. Who was I fooling?

"Burnout is nature's way of telling you, you've been going through the motions your soul has departed... "
Sam Keen

Fortunately, it is possible to overcome overwhelm and avoid burnout. It's also possible to go from burnt to shine when you have the right support.

Think of all the people waiting to be touched by the legacy you're building and then think ten times bigger. You can grow exponentially when you Magnify Your Essence. The world needs you.

It's time to *Dazzle Without The Frazzle!*

About Bolutiwi Aiyesimoju

Bolutiwi is a philanthropreneur, coach for high-achieving women, international speaker, and founder of Magniessence, a global movement inspiring over one million women high-achievers to magnify their essence for more conscious impact.

Her unique path during her 14-year international career in diverse roles at L'Oréal gave her a first-hand perspective of the challenges that high-achievers face.

By the age of 28, Bolutiwi had initiated and created a transformational programme that became one of the most widely attended in the group's history, with over 18,000 people in attendance.

In 2015, the wings of excitement gave way to disillusionment. Bolutiwi, despite her incredible energy, was burning out.

Bolutiwi now inspires and supports high-achieving women to magnify their essence, to grow as leaders liberated from limitation, and to contribute more consciously. She believes that by being more of our true selves, doing less, we're free to shine brighter without burning out.

Contact Bolutiwi Aiyesimoju

IE: https://contactb.me

https://linktr.ee/Bolutiwi

From Debilitating Self-Image To Conquering Your Comfort Zone! How To BE The Difference That Makes The Difference

Claudine Matthews - The Women's Mentoring Magnet

'Every closed door leads you closer to your purpose and power!'

Have you ever prayed for a breakthrough so much that you felt like your life depended on it? Well, my breakthrough came in 2008, at 37 years old. All this time I lived in personal, professional and academic captivity, blind to my own gifts, value, talents, and ability. I was living from a place of disempowerment, low personal value and worth, crippling my potential to achieve.

It was the invitation to my first ever women-in-leadership event that triggered my transformation.The stark reality of my low self-esteem played right out in front of me as I observed these powerful women leaders sharing their achievements and future aspirations. All I could think was, That's not me, I can never be that; I'm not good enough. But today, as I write this story for you as an empowered and transformed mentor and leader who is owning her value, this could be you!

Have you ever heard the phrase time is money? Well, if I were to calculate the monetary value of all the time I've lost whilst living in disempowerment, mediocrity and underachievement,

I would have created multiple 7-figure businesses without even trying! If you resonate with this at all, please stop wasting your time. Learn from my experience and start taking action today.

Don't make the same mistakes I made. If you want to live in total freedom and fulfilment, follow the simple system I am going to share with you here. All you have to do is decide to take one action to change the trajectory of your life, so in this chapter, let's do it together.

Perhaps you are like me and have lived far too long with a debilitating self-image. I know that feeling all too well, as the way I used to see myself was through a limited and disempowered lens, creating a limited reality and a skewered ability to achieve. Spending my formative years in a South African culture, rife with racial discrimination and prejudice seemed to reinforce this personal weakness. These negative experiences seemed to further embed a disempowering mindset that only certain groups of people could achieve at a higher level. So despite having all the potential to do more, reach higher academically, personally and creatively, I limited my achievement and operated well within my comfort zone. I allowed this to define me, stunting my growth, confidence, self-belief and capability to achieve to my highest potential.

The impact of living with a disempowered mindset was evident from an early age. Despite, being a gifted ballet dancer, I literally ran away from an opportunity to step into a principal dancer's role after only two years of dance experience. I was 12 years old, and I never attended another lesson.

At 16, I passed on a second, potentially life-changing opportunity, when I turned down the offer to preach in church, which I never did until many years later in the UK. This level of disempowerment continued way after qualifying as a dietician and limited my overall achievement and vision as a professional and an individual.

Following my graduation, there was an opportunity to do

my Masters in Dietetics, but I did not even contemplate this because I believed I wasn't clever enough. My disempowerment continued until my husband and I decided to emigrate to the UK in 2000. This was followed by my awakening to leadership in 2008, which was life-changing.

For the first time, I started to value myself and wanted more from me. I was starting to transition from living with a disempowered and limited mindset, which for years dictated my thoughts, feelings and behaviours. The unfolding transformation offset a mindset transitioning, taking me from a place of limitation, lack and underachievement, to a compelling desire to broaden my horizons. No longer was I content with the status quo. I wanted to be liberated to explore my potential and develop my confidence as a leader.

Three years after my awakening, I enrolled in a Master's Degree in Leadership. I was finally stepping into my potential and I excelled at it! I was energised by my learning and the mentors who were guiding me; the more I learned, the more I wanted to learn and experienced a physiological boost when I was learning. This was the power of leadership and mentoring, testimony to how my empowered mindset was now positively influencing who I was becoming.

My personal empowerment journey was now propelling my ability to value myself at a much higher level and my mentors had a vital role to play in my development. So much so that I went from underachievement for nearly 38 years to in just the last ten years, successfully completing my Master's in Clinical Leadership, writing over ten published articles, writing my debut book whilst undergoing treatment for cancer and in 2021, achieving my Doctorate. In just the last month alone, I started building the world's largest mentoring platform for women leaders around the globe and I am now published in this book... all because I said yes to myself, which is something I didn't feel worthy to do for the first 38 years of my life. It's amazing what surrounding yourself with great mentors can do!

The bottom line is: if I can, you can.

Remember, you are not alone, I am here to walk you through how to get started!

If you are tired and fed up with wasting your time watching others excel while you keep spinning your wheels, then change can start now. If you are tired of living from a place of disempowerment, stuck in an unfulfilling position, filled with resentment or untapped potential that is causing you to underachieve in every area of your life, then I have proven that it doesn't have to be this way.

As the result of thousands of hours working with patients, colleagues, emerging leaders in the NHS and academia, and my own life experiences, my intention in this chapter is to inspire, empower and equip you to, like me, transition from a place of limited potential to a place of empowerment and achievement.

An old Chinese proverb says every long journey begins with the first step. So I challenge you to take your first step by completing this ASSESS Personal Empowerment Quiz now. This is the first step of a bigger personal empowerment process I designed that will help you to:

- Discover, who you are and the limiting beliefs that hold you back.
- Modify your thinking to change your behaviour and habits.
- Transform your learning and development potential.
- Step out of your comfort zone and do what you've never done before.

However, before you can jump into doing these four things above, let's start at the beginning to reveal whether you are really motivated enough to make the change you want to see in your life, and if not, keep playing with your answers until you come up with a compelling enough reason to go for it!

Let's go...

The ASSESS Model	Quiz Questions	Scale 1 is (Low) 5 is (High)
Attitudes	Q1: On a scale of 1-5, how important is improving your personal empowerment? Why?	
Self-Determination	Q2: On a scale of 1-5, how **motivated** are you to improve your confidence? Why?	
Self–Efficacy	Q3: On a scale of 1-5, how **able** are you to improve your confidence?	
Empowerment	Q4: On a scale of 1-5, how **confident** are you to improve your confidence?	
Self–Responsibility	Q5: What are you already doing to improve your confidence?	
Self–Awareness	Q6: What help do you need to improve your confidence?	

Now let's take a look at your results, as your answers tell you three really important things.

Firstly, knowing where you are prepares you for embarking on your personal empowerment journey by helping you to explore the reasons why your personal empowerment is important to you. Being unclear about your reasons why increases your susceptibility to succumb to life's challenges, preventing you from taking action. If for example, in Q2 you said you are not motivated to improve your confidence, think about what changes you could make, or alternative ideas that would motivate you to turn your answer from a zero into a five.

Secondly, your answers provide the opportunity for you to explore some of the factors that may affect your levels of motivation and ability to improve your confidence levels. This too is critical in providing valuable insights into your overall level of activation that will enable and support your action towards behaviour change. In doing so, you will be in a better position to discover who you are, modify your thinking, transform your learning and step out of your comfort zone.

Knowing where you are in the first step, so congratulations on taking action already!

You, yes you, can step into your vision, your value and claim it, just as I have done. It's time for you to reach your full potential and step into your next level of achievement.

So join me now in being the difference that makes the difference. You will never look back!

About Claudine Matthews

Claudine is the founder of the world's largest mentoring platform for emerging women leaders, advocating the transformation of women's leadership development and achievement. She is the go-to thought leader at Doctorate level, having spent the last ten years establishing herself as a thought leader in personal leadership empowerment. This enabled her to develop the EQ 5 Empowerment System, equipping her to take control of her life, step out of disempowering belief patterns and achieve her highest potential.

Claudine is the author of the upcoming book *Connecting To Your Purpose*, aiming to support millions of women who are desperate to be seen and heard.

Contact Claudine Matthews

claudine@mentoringwomenglobal.com

linkedin.com/in/claudine-matthews-747566b0

www.facebook.com/groups/mentoringwomenglobal

Instagram: @claudinem05

Part Three

Own Your GIFT

From Sabotage To Success
How To Have It All Without Losing Yourself

Aleksandra Rehar - The Manifestation Mentor

"Every step you take is a choice. Don't be afraid to lose, as you are already on your way to winning."

Everything you do in life has a higher purpose. What you do, the lessons you learn and the way you live your life defines who you are as a person. Your dreams are already right in front of you, waiting for you to claim them! But perhaps they are just far enough out of sight that you cannot see the path ahead. Maybe you have lost sight of what you truly want, or perhaps you've been blinded by the fear inside you because past experiences have hurt you.

Ahh yes, that lurking saboteur... always waiting for you to express even the slightest doubt so that your ego can do its job to step in and save you from growing. This is a pattern I know only too well.

From early childhood, all I ever knew was loss and sabotage. First, my sister died, then my brother. My mother followed, along with my apartment and job. This threw me into a pattern of self-destruction, which led to a lifetime of self-sabotage.

My childhood was never easy, and I always felt like I had a real struggle on my hands. It started when a group of bullies targeted me at school, making my life utterly miserable. Then my father became aggressive after my brother died. A negative pattern developed within me and I took on a persona that transformed me into a bitter, angry teenage girl.

This turbulent childhood built within me a fearful and aggressive ego, creating a solid wall around me. I didn't trust anybody except for my mum. I doubted everything and everyone. I was afraid to get hurt by people, so I stayed away from them. This anger was so strong in me that I took it out on the wrong people and before I knew it, I was taking it out on the one person I could trust… my mum. That was until one day she became very sick, and my life would never be the same.

After six months of struggling in hospital, she died. To say it was a huge shock for me was an understatement. I was just 23 years old at the time and after the autopsy, they determined she had died of pancreatic cancer. Another loss, but this time it was different. This time I'd lost the only feeling of security that I'd had.

I thought: Thank God I have a steady job and can pay the bills. But after five miserable years in a 'secure' job I didn't like, I was laid off. That security blanket was gone too now. That job was the only thing I could lean on, but it wasn't enough anymore. Deep inside I could feel the yearning of a higher purpose and the life I was living was not it. It wasn't fulfilling me at all. I couldn't see it at the time, but losing that job was the best thing that could have happened to me. Perhaps you have had moments like this in your life? It is only through looking back that you can see what a blessing it was, hey!

As a child I remember having a vivid vision of me wearing a white business dress with a white hat. My hair was long and curly, and I had high heels on. My big white house was by the ocean and I had it all - financial security and freedom.

I can still see it now as I recall it to you. A part of me always knew this is the life I was supposed to live, but my ego didn't want to believe I could have it all. I was in great denial. I trusted myself so little that I'd rather believe people around me than believe in myself.

My ego wanted me to look for another job to stay safe and I applied for all the jobs I could find on the internet. My intuition was screaming inside me however, that this is not the way. My ego and intuition were in a constant battle, raising a deep sense of unworthiness and distrust within me. All the doors were closed around me and I couldn't understand why.

Until one day I finally crashed.

My thoughts were so deeply dark that the only thing I could think about was ending it all. Suicide felt like my only option. As I stood there with tear-stained cheeks, feeling the lowest I had ever felt, I couldn't decide whether to take the pills or cut my veins. In that moment, I heard a voice in my head, and it was a voice I recognised instantly. It was my late mum. She told me loud and clear: Don't look for a job. Look another way. You won't get any steady job in life, so don't bother with that.

Oh my God! I thought I was insane. I thought I needed to go to a mental hospital. I didn't know what to do. How could it be possible that she spoke to me? I didn't understand it, but after that moment, my visions and the messages I downloaded got stronger. I started to see spirits and hear their voices. Really? can't live like this! It was like a doorway opened and a whole party of people invited themselves through the door without invitation.

I desperately needed to speak to someone I could trust and found a teacher who helped me take control of the voices. For the first time in as long as I could remember, I felt like I was on the right path. Who could know that this would change my career and build me an entirely new life?

After seven years of developing my skills and supporting my clients to live their dream lives, my intuition became the foundation of everything I did.

Before it was my security, but now my intuition underpinned everything. I had been searching for my gift, but it had been within me all along! Following my intuition stopped me from self-sabotaging, while my growing spirituality gave me patience. It calmed me down, helped me to get in control of my anger, and this healed my grieving wounds.

I forgave myself. I forgave my father. I forgave my mother.

I learnt a lot on this journey, but still, I could feel the emptiness. I dived deeper, searching how to get to the next level and continue developing my true life path and gift. I dreamt of working from home and having my own online business. I dreamt of living a good life with lots of freedom to do as I wished. So, how could I have such clear dreams and yet still be struggling?

One day I'd had enough. I took out a piece of paper and wrote on one side: *What do I want in life?* Then on the other side I wrote: *What don't I want in my life?* I got super clear, committed it to paper and swore that I would do anything and everything I could to change my situation. I was ready to create a success of my life... and I did! I even found an incredible business partner too, who started as my mentor and now we are building our dream business together.

My greatest lesson of all? When I became my true self and finally owned my gift of intuition, all of the right people showed up in my life. I realised that all of my life's lessons shaped me into the diamond I am today. After losing everything, I reconnected with the one thing that I had inside me all along - my intuition, my gift.

Your intuition is the only thing you really need, and nobody can ever take it away. When you trust yourself, you become certain of yourself and you realise that it is you who creates your own security, your circumstances, your future, your abundance and everything you see around you. It is all you ever need in life. *It is already within you!*

My ego is now my friend and everything I do today as a coach and mentor starts with uncovering the inner diamond within you. So, here's how you can start to uncover your inner diamond and have it all, without losing yourself along the way.

1. Follow your inner guide. What does your intuition tell you in this moment of the situation you are thinking about most? Whatever your immediate instinct is, that is the true answer.
2. To build your inner strength muscle, dare confidently and trust yourself. You've got this.
3. Acknowledge that you have all answers inside of you already. Your gut is always right.
4. Your life path will go so much easier when you trust yourself. Back yourself – you are worth it.
5. Your intuition will always lead you to the right people and mentors.
6. Your real successes will come easily to you when you follow your heart.

Following these core principles helped me and I know they will help you too when you follow them.

Your dreams will come true when you are finally backing yourself fully. It is when you believe 100% in what you are doing to enrich the lives of others that the results will manifest in every area of your life. You don't need to look for your gift anymore because you are the gift!

Are you ready to live life fully on your terms now?

Yes? Great, then let's go!

About Aleksandra Rehar

Aleksandra Rehar is an international manifestation mentor and in-demand business coach with 11 years' experience supporting small business owners to uncover their gifts and create a clear vision for their business. Her world-renowned programmes and workshops have helped hundreds of people to trust their intuition, guiding them to make better choices in business so they can confidently achieve their dreams and live the fulfilled life they deserve.

Based on her life experiences, she created a unique six-step programme that takes people through a proven process to stop self-sabotage, uncover their true potential and use their own gifts to create the future aligned with who they really are.

Contact Aleksandra Rehar

Email: quantumbusinessleaders@gmail.com

Facebook: https://www.facebook.com/groups/quantumbusinesleaders

Instagram: @aleksandrarehar

The Inner and Outer Game Of Successful Selling

Navin Jaitly - The Inner Game Maximiser

"Work on your inside and the magic will happen on the outside."

I stood at the reception of my client's waiting room. Posh, swanky central London offices. It was a big meeting... make or break for me. I was fairly new both to the world of sales as well as the company I worked for, and hadn't yet sold a thing. I was trying to put on a brave face and act like I was confident in front of the receptionist who was engaging in chit chat with me. I was making small talk with her, laughing and joking. Inside, a very different conversation was going on in my head.

Navin, what if you mess this meeting up?

You're already behind on your sales quota.

Your boss might start losing faith in you.

Maybe you're not cut out for a career in sales.

After all, you only went into sales because everyone else said you would be a natural.

Maybe it's better if you get sacked.

At least you'd be put out of your misery.

This currently feels like daily torture.

At that point, I zoned back into the conversation and pretended to laugh at the receptionist's joke. Next thing I was being greeted by a man in a grey suit. It was my client. He was so much taller than I imagined him to be. He exuded confidence and seemed very serious. A few minutes later, I was sitting opposite him and the meeting was underway. I asked a couple of questions and my client did most of the talking for the first few minutes. I was relieved about this. After about five minutes, the client asked me a question.

I froze. I had suddenly forgotten some very important information about the industry. I couldn't believe it; I blurted out an answer that I just made up on the spot. The client gave me a look of disdain. He asked me another question related to my answer. I froze again and had to admit I didn't know. He then asked me if my original answer had been accurate. I dropped my head in shame and said I thought I'd got it wrong. Again, the inner dialogue went off.

How can you be so stupid?

Why did you make up an answer?

You should have just said you didn't know.

You've lost credibility now.

This guy is in a senior position and he doesn't take fools gladly.

I managed to snap out of my thoughts and zone back into the conversation. As the conversation unfolded, the client seemed to speak less and less; he looked impatient and bored at the same time. I just kept ploughing on with my verbal diarrhoea.

I suddenly remembered the sales training of how to keep a client engaged. Just keep asking him open questions. I got to my third consecutive open question when he suddenly blurted out, *Stop! I think I've heard enough. These questions are irrelevant and frankly speaking, a waste of my time. There's no point continuing this conversation. We won't be buying.*

My heart sunk. This meeting was worse than I had imagined. It was a total disaster, in fact. What went wrong? I followed the sales training, asked the client open questions about his business, sat with confident body language, listened more than I spoke. I went home that night confused, upset and angry with myself. I felt like sending an email to my boss to resign.

Many years have passed since that meeting and I now look back laughing at it. I can honestly say it was one of the best things that happened to me. After that meeting, I had a serious look at what I was doing wrong.

I realised the reason I wasn't selling was not because I didn't have the intelligence, the talent, the desire or the training. It was because of the negative inner dialogue that was going on in my head. The dialogue which I now call the inner game.

A rock-solid inner game is a basic requirement for high performance. This is especially true when it comes to situations where you are required to sell. Whether that be as an entrepreneur selling your service to society, a salesperson selling your product or service to a client, or a public speaker selling your vision to the world.

The Inner Game Process

Elite salespeople have this sussed. The inner game is like the engine of a car. You can have the best body and wheels (outer game), but if the engine doesn't work, the car will go nowhere. This is far too big a topic to cover in one chapter. However, there are a few basic principles to this that I will cover.

I call this the ABCDEF of Inner game ...

Awareness

In order to master performance, you need to be aware of what's holding you back internally. Where's your mind at? What are your limiting beliefs? What are your fears? What do you often think about what's stopping you from getting where you want to go? This first step is vital for you to understand what you need to pay attention to and how you need to develop.

Belief

If you want to sell anything or influence anyone, you need to believe in yourself and your product or service. There can be no doubts. You need complete faith. Belief comes from reminding yourself of all your strengths and successes in life, both big and small. It comes from reminding yourself why you are great. We were all born with greatness but unlearned this greatness when we were first exposed to the world and mainly during childhood. Belief in your product and service comes from truly understanding how and why it will make a difference to your clients' lives.

Clarity

When you know what you want and, more importantly, why you want it your inner game will accelerate. Your decision-making will be sharper, you will no longer feel confused, you won't be pushed around by others. Clarity brings conviction and conviction brings personal power. Even when you are in a disempowered state, your clarity of vision will provide you with the power and conviction to keep going.

Dominate

You must remember that you're a gift and an asset to whoever you're speaking with. If you go into a sales meeting thinking the client is more intelligent, powerful and resourceful, then you will feel fearful. This in turn creates a defensive mindset which is something that will hold you back. You need to go into an interaction viewing yourself as an equal and someone the client should appreciate as you are providing them value. This doesn't mean that you want to dominate them, but rather you want to dominate your own thought process before a meeting.

Empower

As well as strengthening your own inner game when selling, it's vital that you strengthen the inner game of your clients. Often clients want to buy, it's just that they are riddled with more insecurities than the seller. They have fears about getting it wrong. What if I spend too much? What if this product/service doesn't work? What will I tell my boss/husband/wife if this doesn't work out? Clients need empowering to help them make decisions. So, when selling, rather than focusing on trying to impress, focus on their emotions instead. What emotions do they need to feel in order to feel comfortable with the purchase? The question to ask yourself is, *how can you empower them?*

Fear

Must be dealt with in order to allow your mind to be free to sell effectively. There are many types of fear but usually when it comes to sales the most common ones are the fear of rejection, fear of failure and fear of being judged. The best way to deal with these fears is to ask yourself questions like: *Why is it my duty to ensure I convince the client to purchase my product or service? What benefit or problem will the client solve by doing so?*

Making it about your client will take the spotlight away from you. It will relieve the pressure you are putting on yourself and help diminish the fear. Furthermore, ask yourself, *What would I have to be feeling, thinking and doing right now to be the best version of myself?* Asking this question forces, you to work through the fear and show up as your most confident self.

The concepts summarised in this chapter only scratches the surface when it comes to you remembering your gifts, owning your gifts and valuing them. However, just following these simple principles above will provide you with the basic insights needed to work on your inner game.

Performance comes from inside out. Conquer your inner self and you will manifest the success you deserve!

About Navin Jaitly

Navin is an award-winning speaker, salesman and accredited executive coach. He runs Navin Jaitly Coaching Ltd and works with purpose-driven entrepreneurs, corporate executives and business leaders to maximise their performance.

After spending 15 years in corporate sales, he went from under-performer to high-achiever almost overnight, winning multiple sales awards and accolades. He realised that the key to high-performance was working on his beliefs, thoughts, emotions and relationships. Once he developed the tools and techniques to do this, it was a game changer.

After becoming an accredited executive coach, he realised his love was to train and coach people to perform to the best versions of themselves. To help leaders turn around their underperforming teams into highly prized assets.

His mission is to massively impact the performance and lives of over one million people globally through using his inner game methods.

Contact Navin Jaitly:

www.navinjaitlycoaching.com

navinjaitlycoaching@outlook.com

www.instagram.com/navin263

www.linkedin.com/in/navinjaitly

www.facebook.com/navin.jaitly

Self-Sovereignty – Your Key to a Higher Vibe

Jane Butterworth - The Sovereign Frequency Architect

"Everything you plant should have an Intention"

Who am I? What have I got to offer? What do I believe in?

This is the scrutiny you need to apply when creating a business from your dreams and looking to present yourself to the world.

It is critical that you align to your authentic self and gifts because that makes you bombproof. Dreams can be so easily squashed and trampled upon by a well-meaning family member or work colleague. One sentence can go right inside and eat up your motivation and self-belief. To think, one person in seven billion on this planet can prevent you from realising your dream. What is worse, is you allow it.

What if you had a proven method to keep your vibe high and super clear?

Now more than ever, it is vital that you deeply align with your gifts and see them as a frequency thrumming through your veins. Your gift will change someone's life. There is an entrepreneur ascension going on in our world today. Individuals are creating businesses in their bedrooms, huge communities forming out of two people with a cool idea. This is energy at work. A gift living within your energy field is coming forward to be heard and now it is time to give it life. Your dreams are your sovereign gift to the world. The life you want is in the wings, waiting for you to embody it and to take ownership of it.

As I searched for my gifts, I had to work hard on my self-belief, and it took me ten years to realise I did have something to offer people. I do not want you to take that long! I have been in many jobs throughout my life. I have worked for a private investigator, been in fashion wholesale, fashion retail, and even taught ballroom dancing.

Then I was made redundant and was at my lowest. I felt I had wasted my time and not focused on a real career. So I took a course to learn about computers and began a role with an IT company, finding myself happily working in a stable industry. Corporate life is great, guaranteed salary, all the perks and some great folk to work with. Then my world fell apart.

In 2006, my sister was diagnosed with cancer and it was terminal. My family and I spent a year in hospital as she had operations and experimental treatments. By the time she passed over, we were numb and exhausted. I wanted to help her but so felt helpless.

I was also becoming unwell. Endless overtime and hours on the keyboard were affecting my hands. My neck was painful, causing shooting pains in my head. It turns out that you are totally replaceable if the company needs to restructure. It was the catalyst for me to begin my journey. What a gift! I didn't want to just survive, I wanted to thrive.

I learned about many modalities and travelled to beautiful countries meeting amazing people. There was a whole new world out there and it had a vibrant, beating heart. For a while I had a blast, but I was beginning to suffer from shiny objects syndrome, following Guru's, joining groups led by others and absorbing their beliefs. A void inside me was growing and slowly the penny dropped. I needed to align with my own gifts and give them space to emerge.

I listened to my inner voice. I had to find the answers within me, I had to believe I could do this and most importantly, I was going to be OK. The more I focused on finding those core pillars within me, the more I developed an energetic forcefield around me. I could empower myself and navigate my life.

It was a breakthrough. I went on to establish my White Star Lion business. Essential oil blends which are personally coded for your soul journey. Yes, I do that! I ran a successful pilot and have never looked back. I learned a lot about the frequencies of all living things and the information field that we live in.

During this time, a new belief was forming in my mind. That we can heal ourselves with sound and vibration. I was seeing devices being created by scientists that could see our bio-field, measure it and analyse our own bodies requirements. Then to send those balancing frequencies to our bio-energetic field. I began to widen my focus to the area of technology.

I am now marketing a ground-breaking quantum frequency device, new technology for personal wellness in the home. I learn about quantum physics directly from the scientist who created it and share my day with like-minded heart-conscious entrepreneurs.

So how do you become indestructible in your self-belief and yet remain open to new information, continuing to learn and grow? The language of the Universe is sound, light and vibration and your ability to listen to that language is how you engage with your inner guidance. The bio-energetic field of consciousness is all around us and you are a part of it.

Everything vibrates at a certain megahertz; your body, your organs, all have their own resonance, as do your thoughts. Belief systems are based upon past events, they can get fixed at a young age and we don't do so much to try to get those in balance or recognise that they have a powerful influence over us.

Interacting with people can shift your emotions, change your resolve, and alter your decisions. It is in recognising the shift in your vibration that gives you the power to correct yourself. Your very own sovereign energy boundary. Energy flows where your attention goes.

So if you are looking to discover your inner gifts and attract the right tribe to your vibe, you need a dynamic practice to keep your focus super clear and your vibe super high.

The Four Pillars Of Self-Sovereignty

- **V – Vision** – *You are a powerful manifester and creator*
- **I – Inner Journey** – *Continual connection to your ' Divine Compass'*
- **B – Belief** – *Move low vibrational belief energy to high vibrational outcome*
- **E – Empower** – *Amplify your bombproof vision – give it your attention!*

Vision

This is your dream, your talent and the thing that makes you most happy. The Universe responds to feelings. Feel it, be happy for it, see yourself doing it. Do not worry about how it is going to happen, suspend your need to understand and you will shift into creator mode. Also, when you are working from the heart, write down the core values that represent your moral compass.

Such as: Authenticity; Sensitivity; Empathy; Courage; Dynamism; Joy; Creativity; Attentiveness.

Be prepared to view all your values as the *Source* where your gifts can come together to manifest your *Divine Compass* and attract everything you want into your movement.

Inner Journey

This is the route to your gifts, discovering the treasure within. Some you may be aware of and some you may not know are there. I provide these meditations to guide you to this space to tune in to the frequency of who you truly are. Take time to do this inner journey as it is the key. Only you can do this and only you will see what comes up for you. Make space for the thoughts to come into your mind.

Belief

Your subconscious always says yes! Did you know that? So if you are beating yourself up and saying I just can't do this, then your subconscious will agree with you. Identify what holds you back, acknowledge it as part of your being. Then create a balance by identifying your power attributes as well. Energy flows where attention goes. Your subconscious looks for where the power is, and it creates that.

Empower

Focus daily on the energy flow to amplify the gifts you have and move it away from your weak spots, so you are always energising the frequency around your gifts and attracting synchronicity and abundance.

If you generate these pillars, your self-confidence and decision-making begins to amplify and life just gets a lot easier.

Sovereignty comes out of understanding who you are to the point where you acknowledge that you are enough. You have the skills to move forward and if you keep listening, you will be guided along the way. You no longer need to seek the opinions of others to authenticate or validate your gifts.

Sovereignty is a powerful frequency, as you grow in your inner assurance, this frequency oozes from your pores. People begin to listen to you, ask you for help and want to collaborate with you. It is within your gift to generate this frequency by fine-tuning and honing the four pillars above.

Make time to write down what your values are and build your four pillars of sovereignty. The world needs you now and I am looking forward to being inspired by your gifts.

About Jane Butterworth

Jane is a Frequency Architect who believes passionately in thriving through wellness, promoting quantum frequency technology to create vibrant life and cellular health.

During 20 years as an IT professional, Jane began suffering from RSI and then the devastating loss of her sister to cancer was the catalyst to finding a way to transform her own health. This initiated a journey of discovery with over 12 years of study and practice in healing and energy modalities.

In 2016, she realised her dream to build a business as an educator in essential oils.

She is the founder of White Star Lion, a portal for conscious awakening. She provides personally coded essential oil blends which align to powerful activations and meditations. They are specifically designed to empower your personal soul sovereignty.

Jane mentors holistic wellness entrepreneurs to grow their businesses, marketing ground-breaking quantum frequency technology for mind, body, and spirit.

Contact Jane Butterworth

linktr.ee/JaneButterworth

Reawaken Your Purpose

Helen Jane - The Purpose Reawakener

"There is more to life because there is more to you."

I remember it as if it were yesterday, the surgeon saying, "If you go back to your job, you'll suffer severe and chronic back pain".

It was one of those moments when life stands still. I felt sick, as if I were in a nightmare wishing I could wake up.

Looking back, I now see that my life was falling apart so I could reawaken my purpose. My gift was there all along, I just wasn't tapping into it.

I had been a single mum working full-time and studying for a degree in psychology. I loved my job working at Manchester Airport for British Airways. It was hardworking shifts while bringing up my son, but life was good. I'd been taught to believe you had to work hard.

When my son was twelve, I met the love of my life - or so I thought. The relationship was good for the first few years, but then I started to get a nagging feeling that something wasn't right. I didn't want another failed relationship to add to my collection and did everything I could to make it work, but how could it? I was involved with a liar and cheat - again!

Within months of the relationship breakdown, I was made

redundant from my job and transferred to long-haul cabin crew at Heathrow. My son, who was 17 at this point, went to live with his dad as I was away from home all the time working. I was devastated.

I could sense my life starting to unravel. I hated the job, commuting and being away from home. I ignored my inner voice and carried on for a few more months, at which point I was forced to stop and listen. Whilst at work, I suffered a serious back injury resulting in surgery. After 25 years, I had to resign from BA not knowing what I'd do next. It was terrifying. Some days the pain was excruciating. Those were the days I found it hard to carry on.

Over the next few years, things went from bad to worse. I was forced to sell my home as I couldn't pay the mortgage. I was made redundant five times. My mum was diagnosed with dementia, my son emigrated to New Zealand and finally, my mum passed away. Some days I felt there was no point getting out of bed, I had no future and started to ask questions:

Is this all there is?

What is my purpose now?

There must be more to life, surely?

I realised I'd spent all my life looking after others and neglecting myself, putting their needs before my own. It was my time now. Instead of seeing a big, empty void in front of me, it was time to create the life I wanted to live. It was time to put myself first and listen to what I wanted to do. I began to see that life was happening for me, not to me.

Does this sound familiar to you?

Despite the pain, I'd been given so many gifts. I've always loved to learn and now it was time to start sharing my gifts, knowledge and life experience with others, supporting them so they didn't make the same mistakes. My pain turned out to be one of my greatest gifts. Perhaps the same is true for you?

I now know my purpose is to teach and share. I feel as if I have reawakened from a long slumber and reconnected with the purpose I kept buried for so long. Now is the right time. I'm happy to embrace new beginnings and as I do so, new opportunities are coming to me. I've reconnected to my values and life is good.

Hundreds of women I know have spent so long taking care of others that they have neglected themselves. Many of these women have had successful careers, raised and supported their children to be independent and courageously follow their dreams. They've supported their partners and husbands to create successful careers, maybe even cared for elderly parents. They have lived their lives according to expectations of others and/or society.

Others have chosen to follow a different path. They've worked hard and built successful careers in male-dominated professions because they've been taught this is how success should look. They may have spent many years pushing themselves to be their best, terrified they will appear weak or inferior if they don't. This results in many losing touch with their core and femininity. On the outside, they seem to have it all, but do they? What have they sacrificed to build the 'perfect life'?

Something interesting happens at midlife. We start to re-evaluate life. We start searching. We start asking questions:

Is this all there is?

What is my purpose now?

There must be more to life, surely?

Far from being a midlife crisis, I see it as a midlife awakening. The opportunity to re-address the balance in your life. The opportunity to change things that no longer serve you. The opportunity to put yourself first. The opportunity to live the life you choose to live, not the life others choose for you.

You may feel discontentment, frustration and yearning for something else starting to bubble up. It's as if you are starting to reawaken from the long sleep. Starting to reconnect to you - the most important person in your life.

"But isn't it selfish? It has been so long. I don't know where to start and even if I did, what would others think?" I hear you ask.

The valid reasons to not listen come pouring into your mind: "Probably best not to rock the boat. Life is ok as it is.

What if it all goes wrong? It's probably better to stay as I am."

Here's the thing: one of your brain's key functions is to keep you safe. It's not always easy to step outside your comfort zone into the unknown. You don't have a reference point for doing things differently. That's why so many of us live habitual lives and avoid risk. In addition to this, you have been conditioned from birth by your parents, family, friends, and society to live a certain way. There is evidence now to suggest that we are influenced in the womb and even by patterns handed down from past generations. It takes courage, self-belief, and persistence to make changes.

You try to ignore that inner voice, but the voice starts to get louder and louder. It starts keeping you awake at night. You distract yourself and keep yourself busy. Still, there it is gently calling you, reminding you of who you are and who you are here to be:

Is this all there is?

What is my purpose now?

There must be more to life, surely?

The questions persist. Perhaps situations and events start to happen in your life to draw your attention to the fact that you are not living a fulfilling, aligned life.

You may fall ill, lose your job, or just feel like running away.

If you are at a crossroads in your life, here's a shortened version of an activity I use with my clients that will help you to start exploring your purpose and gifts. Grab a cuppa, a beautiful journal, a pen and spend some time responding to my prompts below. It may help you to light a candle, put on some relaxing music or even to find a place outside in nature to write.

Don't worry if nothing comes at first. There's no pressure, just take your time, enjoy the process, and revisit it often.

- *What did you enjoy doing as a child and/or young adult?*
- *What brings you joy in life?*
- *What do you lose track of time doing?*
- *If money was no problem, how would you spend your days?*
- *What are your skills and values?*
- *What have you always wanted to learn?*
- *What do you want to be remembered for?*

Living life out of alignment is exhausting, overwhelming and leads to stress, depression, and burnout. Perhaps your physical or mental health is deteriorating. Maybe you don't see the point anymore. These are signs that you're living out of alignment. Going through the motions. Not listening to your inner voice. The voice that's trying to encourage, support and guide you to make changes that are aligned with your gifts and purpose. The voice you are doing your best to ignore.

I have been there. I know what you are going through. I feel your pain. I thought life was good, but then it was like a domino effect as it fell apart. Looking back, I could see the signs, but I chose to ignore them.

Don't let that be you. Take this book as a sign that now is the time to reawaken your purpose, own your gifts and remember there is more to life, because there is more to you!

About Helen Jane

Helen is a certified Energy Alignment Mentor, a transformational coach and qualified clinical hypnotherapist.

Over the last ten years, Helen has worked with hundreds of people to overcome stress, anxiety and depression through her work at MIND and other organisations. She has written and delivered numerous courses to help others to reduce stress and anxiety, to build confidence and self-esteem and to live a more mindful life.

Helen coaches and mentors individuals and groups to facilitate transformation and change. As a founding Energy Alignment Method mentor, Helen is passionate in her work guiding women to set themselves free from the expectations of others and society to rediscover themselves.

Helen works 1:1 with clients and runs personal development groups for women, empowering them to step into their power, working on their energy, mindset and limiting beliefs to reawaken their purpose and get the most out of life.

Contact Helen Jane

hello@helencjane.co.uk

www.facebook.com/helencjane

www.linkedin.com/in/helencjane

Value Your Gifts Within

Sunita Koshal - The Abundance Illuminator

'It's all about the Sparkles! When you release your inner sparkles, you shine a light on the magic and abundance in your life, and for those around you."

It's time to get up, but I don't want to. I'm laying in bed with that familiar sinking feeling in my stomach again. The previous night, I tried to transfer some funds to my daughter studying overseas, only to find that an unexpectedly higher than usual direct debit for my mobile phone had cleared out my bank account. I got on the phone immediately, but no amount of ranting and raving was going to alter the situation. I was furious with myself for being in this position again! When was I going to sort it out?

Eventually I get up as the rest of the family is waiting to start the day. I come back after the school run and sit in the car completely frozen, unable to move, hear or think, totally cut off from every sensation, motivation, everything. Once everyone gets out of the car, it becomes my place to sit and think. There's something incredibly still about this moment. Maybe it's the absence of all external noise, just being in a vacuum, and in the state I am in... it's exactly where I need to be.

As I sit there just staring at my hands on the steering wheel, snippets of memories came back to me. I reflect on my glorious childhood in the sunshine. I am drawn back to my childhood home on the outskirts of Nairobi and the Game Reserve. To keep us safe, my father had built a brick wall to enclose the house. My cousins and I used to scramble up on the wall at the back of the garden and sit there in the afternoon sun whilst our mothers had a nap after lunch. We'd dream our dreams about what life was going to be like when we were grown-up... obviously full of magic, freedom and joy, not constrained by the boring rules that grownups made for us.

Did you ever think, *When I grow up, everything is going to fall magically into place?* Because that's what happens. Did you say to yourself, *I will be in control of my life?* Or did you expect challenge after challenge? When you met and overcame a challenge, did you think, *This is it, I have turned the corner,* then hit Groundhog Day and feel like you are back to square one?

After my second child, we moved back to New Zealand and I wanted to recreate the perfect lifestyle that I'd had as a child. I wanted to give them a magical childhood and I wanted the perfect job, one that would create an abundant lifestyle for them. I was searching for the abundance outside in the world, thinking the value and gift were all out there. And each time, the money I was chasing was never enough. I missed the children growing up because I thought money would solve everything.

As I sit there in the car, I recall the constant rushing. *Come on, hurry up, I have to get to work on time. Don't make me late.*

I was never fully present at work because I was thinking about the children, rushing home to get them bathed, fed and put to bed. We were going to work at creating a secondary income to supplement the first.

I was continually looking for the next thing that would fill that little niggle in my stomach, the need for security, including financial security. The money or the lack of it, made me think less of myself and my ability to provide stability and also the magic for my family. I couldn't see the gifts I already had or allow myself the gift of time to spend with my growing family.

I had spent my whole life following that dream... chasing the next perfect opportunity. I thought the answer was to get a better-paid job. Along the way, we even tried our hand at running a business, which didn't quite work out. That's another story in itself! Yet again, I decided to move the family across the world because I was offered another amazing job with a good salary. This time was going to be it, enabling us to finally have that abundant lifestyle I felt my family deserved. But it was long hours, leaving my now-growing family to fend for themselves.

After I was made redundant, I decided to go into business for myself again, and because by now I knew my mindset was important, I delved into the personal development field with network marketing. Once again, I was spending long hours trying to build a business to recreate the income we had, and my children sorted out their own battles. Although I was working, I was still juggling family, time and money.

So now I find myself back on that anxious day, sitting in the car, angry with myself and the unfairness of it all. The crazy thing is I *still* didn't get it. My solution was to find an even better-paid job, trading my time and my family for even more money. I was working long hours, leaving home before 7am and getting back often after 9pm. I'd arrive home exhausted, crawling into bed late and then get up early to start all over again.

It is true that the Universe keeps on nudging you onto your path and if you ignore the nudges, they get bigger until they stop you in your tracks! Despite numerous situations where I was given the opportunity to stop and re-evaluate, eventually I had no choice. Fortunately, it was only shoulder surgery, but it meant that I couldn't travel to work, and if I wasn't working, I wasn't earning.

It was at this point that I was introduced to the energy modality that started me on the journey of truly understanding my gift and the knowing that actually abundance in my life did not depend on money. When I finally allowed that awareness in allowing myself to recognise the true wealth, gifts and abundance that

I already had in my life, everything else fell into place. Money or lack of it no longer felt like the black hole of failure and now, somehow everything is taken care of. There is freedom of choice.

I would like to leave you with a simple exercise to reflect on.

In order to step forwards into a more abundant, expansive life, it is important to have the clarity and awareness of where you are now.

Choose just one area of abundance to focus on - money, time, joy, health, energy.

Imagine that you are stepping out into a garden, and this garden represents the abundance you see all around you.

Feel your feet on the earth, the solidity of the ground beneath you, holding you and supporting you. Perhaps there is a gentle breeze blowing, you can feel the warmth of the sunlight on your face and hear the birds singing.

Close your eyes, take a deep breath in, getting a sense of where you are in your body. Become present.

Now as you open your eyes and look around, what are you seeing? What is growing in this garden? How many plants are there? Are they seedlings, young plants, lush and vibrant or are some withered and dying? Do they need more sunlight, water, are they being choked by weeds? Are there some in the garden that you don't want but there is an abundance of them... and they just keep on coming back again and again. Is the garden well-maintained, or does it look overgrown?

Of course, this is a reflection of the abundance we see in our lives, and also what you focus on. Do you see an abundance of abundance, or an abundance of lack?

How does this awareness feel?

I will leave you with just one of the ways in which I guide my clients to release how this feels in their energy, so you can begin to shift and own your value, your gifts and the key to your abundance.

Become aware of how your energy feels, take a deep breath in. Pause and as you breathe out, set the intention to release all that doesn't serve you from your energy field, seeing it disintegrating into the ether. Repeat this at least twice more until you feel lighter.

Next take a deep breath in, filled with love, light, expansion and joy. Pause, setting the intention for it to permeate all the cells of your body re-energising and filling them up with light. Repeat this at least twice more with awareness

Journal what you have discovered.

Repeat the exercise.

There is only abundance all around you. The abundance you see is created by what you focus on, your thoughts, beliefs and how you perceive your own value and gifts to be. So be mindful to focus on what you want, be the gift for others and in being the gift, your gift will attract more gifts!

About Sunita Koshal

Sunita is one of the first 22 Energy Alignment Method Mentors worldwide, an Akashic Records Consultant, and Master Abundance Oracle Card Reader. Sunita empowers women to realise the abundance and gifts in their life, raise their wealth consciousness and connect with their inner light and sparkle.

Since 2017, Sunita has worked with hundreds of people at events, group programmes and individually, to transform their energy, mindset, limiting thoughts and beliefs. In 2018, after 40 years, she decided to get off the hamster wheel in the corporate world and pursue her passion to empower others to Illuminate the abundance around them and create a magical life of expansion and joy they love.

Sunita has a calm, intuitive energy and will light your way forwards into abundance with ease and grace. She is a wife and mum to grown-up children and a gorgeous Goldendoodle.

Contact Sunita Koshal

abundancesparkles@gmail.com

www.theabundanceilluminator.com

www.facebook.com/groups/AlignAbundanceSparkles

https://www.instagram.com/sunitakshl

Part Four

Own Your IMPACT

From Monster Mum
To Legacy Luminary
How One Decision Can Skyrocket
Your Impact And Legacy

Téa Staegemann - The Legacy Luminary

"You can either face your demons and change the course of history, or you can let those demons haunt your legacy for generations to come. The choice is always yours."

I could hear the giggles and chatter above the blaring music as I walked upstairs towards my children's bedroom. It sounded like they were having a fun disco, which was slightly concerning as they were only three and five years old at the time. I slowly opened the bedroom door when suddenly, without warning, my mind went blank as I took in the bomb site of mess strewn about the room. Before I knew it, I was filled with what I can only describe as uncontrollable rage. I saw red as I angrily scooped up the books and toys, throwing them all down the stairs while I screamed at my kids, losing emotional control completely.

I swung around angrily from my position on the landing and looked back towards my children, ready to launch into my usual barrage of discipline. I was met with two sets of terrified eyes staring back at me. Bottom lips and bodies trembling, they'd gone from complete joy to being too afraid to speak.

My heart sank and a groan escaped from my mouth as my world came crashing down.

They are afraid of me.

What have I done?

What have I become?

How did we get here?

Oh, dear God in heaven, I need help.

I have become a monster.

I am monster mum.

Most of us will inevitably come head-to-head with a variety of challenges as we go through life, some such as this when you feel like you have lost control of the situation. Whether it's in the boardroom or your kid's bedroom, whilst you may not think about the impact of how you are being in that moment, it's something that can leave a lasting negative impact and therefore, a legacy for all the wrong reasons.

With work and business shifting more to working from home amid the chaos of everyday life, our families are now being exposed to more *stuff* than ever before.

That fateful afternoon on the stairs, I sank to my knees sobbing, realising I had come almost full circle from the trauma and anger I experienced in my own home growing up. I had promised myself I'd never repeat the patterns and pain I witnessed as a child. Over the years, I tried to out-work it, out-perform it, forget it, and stay as far away from my family as possible to avoid the confrontation of it. I tried therapy for years and resigned to the fact that I had issues. Little did I know, all you needed to add to the mix was a busy home, demanding career and some kids – hey presto! The perfect Molotov cocktail ready to explode.

Did all of this *behind-the-scenes* stuff impact my business?

You bet it did! So if you are serious about making a lasting, positive impact, it's time to own who you really are so you can be who you need to be to make the impact you want to make.

"But where do I even start?" I hear you say!

My answer to you is this… don't do what I did and leave it all to fester, allowing yourself to get dragged along by the rollercoaster of emotions, bad attitude and stinking thinking that got you here. I never want you to find yourself, like I did, curled up in bed, seven months pregnant and hopelessly depressed by the state of your life. What I did was get help.

I was so sick and tired of being angry, emotional, depressed and burdened with my past. I didn't deliberately choose to be monster mum, but thank God, after I got help, I was able to own my gift and choose to be someone else. It was no longer optional. I couldn't be the victim and hero of this story, so I simply had to own it all. Yes, even the ugly bits. It wasn't easy, but I knew if I owned it, it was mine to change and shape as best I could. I was ready to go from victim to victor, so I put my big girl pants on and began this journey of a lifetime.

Please understand, I don't for a minute believe everyone needs to go through such pain to create the change you want to see in your life. One of my biggest realisations was that when you blame others, it disempowers you from creating the future you want and becoming the person you really want to be. I also learned you can bypass so many painful mistakes if you allow yourself to be teachable and open to mentoring.

Sadly, many of us avoid the pain associated with facing our demons, so we live in denial until we come face to face with the consequences of our actions or look back on our legacy far too late. However, your legacy cannot be left to chance. You cannot sit on the sidelines while life plays out before you. The game of life isn't won by spectators, it's won by the players. Will you choose to play or spectate?

I choose to play. I want my kids to look at me and say,

my mum owned it. She ran towards the pain and beat the crap out of it. She was strong despite the obstacles she faced.

You too, get to light that torch for your clients, your children and your children's children. You get to be the one who consciously, deliberately and intentionally creates the positive, lasting legacy you leave behind one day. Isn't that an incredible thought?

My own childhood memories and the fear in my children's eyes that day on the stairs, ignited within me the desire to find the tools and create a roadmap I could use to achieve lasting, positive change. I soon realised that legacy was way more than what you do with your life. It's firstly who you are being and secondly, How you are showing up for yourself and others every day.

As humans, we have become so fixated on our doing that we've completely missed the importance of being. I don't mean 'being' as in getting quiet and not performing. It's about the deliberate choices you make and actions you choose to take in a conscious way. It's about owning who you are at the same time as being who you choose to be.

I found it difficult to get the balance right at first, so I created a simple nine-step framework that I've now used for the last five years. It helps me diagnose where in my life I need to focus my attention every day, so I can achieve balance and bliss in my being while making the impact I want to create in the world.

When you focus on how you are being, it sets the stage for intentional living and greater impact. The framework focuses on four key areas of your inner world, the bridge between those worlds and the four key areas of your outer world. It has become the Life Code I live by and measure my legacy against.

As a special gift to you, I created the super simple L.E.G.A.C.Y. tool below that you can use immediately to start creating your intentional and lasting impact. Remember, to attract what you want in your life it all starts with you being who you need to be to attract it. When you answer these questions, you can quickly define which areas are most important for you to focus on first.

1. Leadership

Where do you need to step up and *be* the leader in your life?

2. End in Mind

What does your true legacy look like right now?

3. Greater Good

How versed are you in your truth?

4. Awareness

How are you showing up each day?

5. Conduct

Are you currently living by your rules and does it show?

6. Youth

What's in your past that's still tripping you up?

I used to think legacy is achieved through work and what you leave behind for others. I now know legacy is what you look back to when you are privileged to grow old. No one sits back and smiles about a life crippled by pain, anger, resentment, and unfulfilled dreams. Rather, it's the joy you experience as your life comes to an end, knowing you owned your life, made an impact and lived as best you could.

Both you and I can get up each morning and set in motion our actions towards becoming the pioneers our future generations will thank. Our ripple of impact will be felt by simply choosing to be who we want to be.

Now if that doesn't inspire you, I'm not sure what else will!

About Téa Staegemann

Téa Staegemann is a podcaster, speaker, and creative problem-solving force behind RippleFEST™ and The Visionary Hub™. She is a seasoned entrepreneur, mother of three daughters, and partners a property development business with her husband of 22 years.

Having witnessed first-hand the impact that unresolved trauma, unfulfilled potential and incongruence can have on family, Téa has worked relentlessly over the past eight years to heal her own childhood traumas, while successfully changing her generational patterns and behaviours. She's developed a resilient, empowered outlook with which she approaches life and business as a result.

Tea's life work is to be a voice for change, the champion of personal truth, and create a legacy of wellbeing for future generations. Her superpower is her empathic, intuitive understanding of human nature and behaviour in its highest and lowest forms. Her passion is sharing it simply and understandably with the world through her writing and speaking

Contact Téa Staegemann

www.teastaegemann.co.uk

tstaegemann@me.com

www.facebook.com/tea.staegemann

Instagram.com/tea_staegemann

Miracles Through Movement
All The Answers Are Held In Your Body

Donna Riley - The Miracles Through Movement Mentor

"Your body is the most exquisitely designed organism on the planet, and nothing will ever surpass it. You are a true miracle walking on this earth!"

It starts with a whisper, a sensing that we are being given a message from God/Universe/Source. Your body feels open, relaxed, and calm. There is a feeling of alignment with your truth.

One of my first experiences of this happened when I was very young. I had a vision of myself up on stage sharing my story, my insights on life, and the wisdom I'd acquired from overcoming many challenges. The audience was captivated, hanging on my every word. I felt that collective energy directed toward me and received it into my body. I sensed the vibration reverberate in my cells and emanate back out to them. I was exhilarated and completely in alignment with my purpose. I knew I was fulfilling my destiny.

Perhaps you've had similar intuitive messages. Something inside of you yearns for more than your current situation.

The expansiveness of my vision was in direct contrast to the reality I was living and therefore, it seemed highly unlikely that I would ever come anywhere close to bringing it to fruition.

I was the only girl with three brothers in a conservative Catholic family living in a town of 40,000 people. The dynamic in the family made it clear that I was lesser than because I was a girl. I never felt like I belonged there. My thoughts, viewpoints, and beliefs were different than much of what I was being taught.

On top of that, my highly sensitive nature was not understood by anyone around me. I *knew* there was more to experience beyond my situation. I felt the presence of God/Spirit/Universe through me and in me. Why did we have to go to a building on Sunday in order to connect to our Source? Why did we have to follow some random rules that someone else made up? Why was I criticized for simply being me? Why did everyone think something was wrong with me because I was filled with energy and always wanted to be moving? How could they not understand the human body is meant to move? It was all so confusing.

Looking back now, I understand that's why my soul decided to leave the planet. Nothing made sense here. I didn't fit in. I believed no one understood me and I certainly didn't understand them. So at the age of 12, I manifested a Near Death Experience (NDE). I remember hovering above my body, observing the nurses trying to 'save my life'. I put this in quotes because in that moment, I didn't understand what they were doing. I was so ready to transcend this physical realm. My mother was standing at the end of the hospital bed absolutely terrified, believing she was watching her daughter die. *Mom, it's okay! I am so happy and excited! I want to leave!*

Have you ever felt like you don't fit in and/or have thoughts that you don't want to be here? Do you walk around day to day feeling like there has to be more to life and knowing that you are meant for something bigger? Oh boy, I get it!

For the next 35 years, I never told anyone about that experience. My life became one of adapting and playing small in an effort to be liked and accepted - I had zero self-esteem and self-worth.

Are you playing small in your life?

Do you know your worth?

Now, I know I was operating from the trauma response of fight, flight, or freeze. The world was scary for me. I spent years alone isolating myself and had very few intimate relationships. I was told I was too deep, too intense, too loud, too bossy, basically, just too much. My body was in a constant state of restlessness. It was literally painful to sit still. My only salvation was dance and movement.

I discovered so much about myself and connected to my essence by diving deeper into my body. Dancing was a way to express my feelings or a way to shift them. There were some days where I would spend hours moving in the way my body wanted and waiting for something to heal or be revealed. The whispers became louder and manifested themselves as pain or injuries in my body.

You are destined for more.

You are not meant to work for someone else.

You need to stop pretending your gifts are no big deal!

I heard the message, but my lack of healed trauma prevented me from stepping in. Are you aware that new research shows that up to 80% of pain in the body has an emotional root cause?

By my late thirties, I was fiercely independent, working hard to support myself and took pride in not needing anyone. On the surface, it looked like I had it all together. Inside, I was a mess. I wonder if you can relate to having imposter syndrome and knowing that you are living in such a way that you are not aligned with your truth? The whispers had become louder and now they turned into screams.

It was the last day of a four-day meditation workshop. I was having a very different experience than everyone else in the room. While all the other participants were blissing out, I was seeing only darkness, murder, war, fire, chaos. There was not one single peaceful or beautiful image. During the final meditation, the white Light from my NDE appeared in the foreground. The darkness was still there, but the Light prevailed.

"Wow", I thought, "I am being shown the extremes of Light and Dark all in one image. Now, I understand. It's time to do some healing around the moment I faced death."

Over the next four days, I had what I call an energetic meltdown. I started to vibrate, couldn't eat, and felt drunk. Once again, I looked to my body for the answer. I discovered that I was really pissed for being here! All of a sudden, my whole life made sense!

It made sense why I was always agitated and restless.

It made sense why my motto was nobody gets it.

It made sense why I had no desire to connect with other humans.

It made sense why I never thought about what I like and what I wanted.

I had no idea the answers I was seeking outside of myself were actually living in the tissues of my body!

Are you aware of what trauma, fear, or stress is being held inside of you?

Do you believe any pain or limitation in your body is just because you are getting older and there's not much you can do about it?

I'm here to tell you that's just not true!

Fast forward to the age of 56, when through my own fascia release and movement practice, I had a soul retrieval experience where my 12-year-old self showed up to reclaim the parts of myself that I had left behind. Finally, I am fully present and alive in my body! I have zero pain or restrictions and I now move through life with ease and grace. I now listen to the whisper before it becomes a scream.

After all the things I have been through in this life, there is absolutely one thing I know for sure. The path to becoming the highest version of yourself and feeling amazing in your body at any age is the journey home to yourself. One of the greatest skills you can develop is to understand how to listen to the wisdom of your body and take action that is aligned to your truth.

I spent most of my life escaping to the Light. Now I know t he real quest is to bring the Light into the body.

My passion is to mentor women to raise the consciousness that lives within and to move their bodies in such a way that they are being the movement, as opposed to doing the movement!

Are you ready to move to a place of openness, expansiveness, and possibilities?

Here are three tips I recommend for getting you started:

1. **Connect to your breath from a new perspective.**
   Your breath is the basis of expansion and contraction.
   The more you can inhale, the more you can take in the goodness of life and create space in the body. When there is space, you can be more connected to your intuition. Your capacity to exhale, is correlated with your ability to release the blocks and limitations that no longer serve you.

2. **Discover the yes and no in your body.**
   Simply ask your body to show you a yes and a no.
   Notice the feelings and sensations that come up with each one.

3. **Whenever you are moving your body, be open to the miracles that await you!** As you make the choice to step into your calling, know the fears, limiting beliefs, and past traumas may show up as pain or tension in your body. See this as a gift. Pay attention, listen, and by all means KEEP MOVING!

About Donna Riley

Donna Riley is a gifted, intuitive movement mentor and inner transformation leader. Her purpose is to awaken, inspire, and empower women to alchemize their pain into pleasure.

This is a deeply personal mission for Donna because after having a Near Death Experience at the age of 12, she has dedicated the rest of her life to learning how to be fully embodied and enjoy this three-dimensional world.

For the past thirty years, Donna has studied movement science, energy medicine, personal development, epigenetics, and other healing modalities. She has the gift of clairvoyance and therefore can see the body in a multi-dimensional way. Donna is able to identify the missing link that is the key to unlocking the limitations, roadblocks, and challenges that prevent women from fully embracing their divine essence and moving through life with grace and fire!

Contact Donna Riley

https://sociatap.com/Donna_Riley

www.instagram.com/miraclesthroughmovement

Getting Ready to ROAR
A Father's Entrepreneurial Journey
From FAILURE to VICTORY

Daniel Wood - The Victory Trailblazer

"'Look to the wind, feel the breeze in your mane and smile as you take another step", said the Lion to his son as they stood together on pride rock.

As entrepreneurs, we live in a world of constant change. We adapt and evolve continually, taking stress in our stride to become the shock absorber for every hard knock that comes our way. There are awesome days where we celebrate hard! Then there are other days that you just want to forget it ever happened. But mostly, you just take it all on the chin and carry on, right?

With so much change happening in our daily work and home life, plus the additional pressures of juggling family, it is no wonder that stress is costing our healthcare systems billions every year. Perhaps, like many people who care about others, you are also experiencing the tension in your body as you keep up with expectations and daily frustrations that are building up, like a pressure cooker inside you, waiting to blow.

As a parent and especially a father, I believe that my role, and the role of every father, is to be the foundation that our future generations can build on. However, if we continue to build on a foundation of stresses and pressures, our tempers are not the only things that are going to blow.

I know I have felt the pressure of living in a world of continuous change, requiring the ability to adapt and evolve quickly. Every day, I see our inability to master change ourselves is negatively affecting not only our businesses, but our children as they suffer the impact of our shortening moods and shortcomings.

There is a positive dynamic in the world where women are gathering momentum and becoming strong leaders. As fathers, we have a choice to accept that our role and impact is evolving or be left behind.

Our most incredible opportunities as parents lie not in always getting it right, but in bouncing back when things go wrong. The innate capability we all have access to is an awesome tool; a weekly, simple, easy-to-do practical activity that gets results. Now is your chance to lead your children in more than just coping with life but excelling in it. It's a tool that every parent can use! However, I am especially keen as a father to get dads all over the world using it after seeing such significant results with my own children.

It's time to be a tremendous leader in this world of change.

When children are born, men become fathers and life gains a new meaning. We are no longer the only ones impacted by our ways; our children are too. Daughters and sons are gaining severe mental and physical health issues because their fathers haven't sorted themselves out yet. I got that understanding when my two daughters and son were young, before I went on an entrepreneurial journey to build my brand.

The world's opinions on how fathers are supposed to be are many and strong. I became a father for the first time in 2001. Striving to meet these expectations led to a mental breakdown as I realised I was failing. I wanted to be the *big earner.*

I graduated with an MBA (a qualification I thought I had to achieve to be successful). I bought a house, had a wonderful wife, three fantastic children, a solid income and perspectives for my career. I had ticked all the boxes.

Then I dreamt of becoming a hero for my family. I wanted to be an entrepreneur. My ambitions were to break free of a life model I saw as a trap. I didn't want to feel like I was one of the 'sheep'.

That went very wrong!

One day, I woke up living on a shop floor, depressed, drowning my sorrows in cheap red wine, no longer living with my children and on course to divorce. Trying to earn money delivering newspapers was not going well either.

Stuck in a pit of desperation, disappointment, depression and despair, the lyrics of a well-known song reminding me how sons will often turn out like their dads haunted me. My emotions were intense as life had stripped me of everything. There was nothing but that feeling of being a complete *failure.*

These words kept running through my mind on repeat:

Frustrated,

Alone,

Insecure,

Lost,

Uncertain,

Regretful,

Existing.

Shortly before my world said *enough*, I learned a simple process now known as TAP. This was and is a simple, practical, easy-to-do activity that I could do on that miserable shop floor. It became the most life-changing action I could take to turn my life around. Regular practice enabled my body to release the tension stored in my core, full of the stress that had for months caused severe back pain and contributed to my depression.

With time, I crawled my way out of my *failu*re and that shop floor. My experience enabled a direction of personal growth on my way to *victory* and the TAP has become a power tool for my three children as they grow into young adulthood.

How Do You Make A Positive Impact On Your Children?

The Lion image standing on Pride Rock looking into the wind caught my eye. I saw how he smiled, knowing he had travelled his path, proud of who he was and his life journey. I wanted that feeling. The image of the VICTORY LION has given me direction ever since. Every mini success is a pride moment, my son and I savour them with a lion pose.

TAP integrated into the ***Total Release Experience***® programme, is easily learnable and your power tool to lead your children. Wherever you are at, turning your life around to a path of VICTORY starts with the simple activity that we now teach all over the world.

The VICTORY LION evolved from seeking a way to put all the words of wisdom I have read and heard into a context to use, make progress and lead my son with. The Lion image smiling with pride spoke to me as the feeling to embrace when I have done something well . Celebrate your successes, however big or small.

The grand goal is to have moments that are worthy of a ROOOOAAAAAR! Being able to stand for who you are and be a father inspiring your children. However, I also use these VICTORY LION principles in my business too!

Here's how you can do it too...

The Four Principles Of Being A Lion

- **L**ove the adventure. Everything you experience serves the goal of a raucous ROAR.
- **I**ntuition is your guiding force. It is nobody else's ROAR but your own.
- **O**vercome internal blockades, barriers, and challenges. Nobody can deal with your stuff. It's your responsibility.
- **N**ever give up. Even if you feel stuck, alone, or lost, you may perceive yourself as a failure, but it's part of your journey – rise to the challenge.

The Seven Areas To Master On Your Road To The Victory Roars

- **V**oice mastery is critical. Whatever comes out of your mouth impacts your children, your life, and others. I have met so many adults who were messed up by their parents' words as children.
- **I**nspire by example. Lay the foundations for your children through your actions, not just your words. The power tool to inspire and lead in a stressful world is to *Thoughtfully Activate the Psoas.*
- **C**ourageously engage with your discomforts. Face your fears, or at least keep chiselling away at them. Ignore the mindset of avoiding stress through caution. It blocks personal growth. Have the courage to stand up and say, *This is where I am going! What is your role in me getting there?*
- **T**ales of overcoming your FAILUREs and when you rise up are well worth listening to. If you're not in a good place, then that's the best place to start telling your story.
- **O**penness to Opportunities that are all around you. Opening your eyes to see beyond the rubbish on your surface is what changes your life dynamic.

- **R**eminders to be Remembered by. Maintaining positive habits that inspire to follow and build upon.
- **Y**esses and Yokes are your choices and core beliefs. Make conscious decisions and gain clarity on what you believe gives you sovereignty. Choose to believe in the VICTORY LION and choose to follow its way.

Now, What Is Worthy of Your ROAR?

- **R**eleases when you allow yourself to let go of the past, enjoy the present and embrace the future.
- **O**bjectives that are fulfilled when you achieve your goals.
- **A**wesomeness moments when you go beyond your comfort zone.
- **R**ealisations in every moment that you gain a new level of self-mastery.

I invite you to join me and play on the path to becoming a VICTORY LION. Your son(s) will love your leadership and your daughter(s) will have a new standard to compare their future partners with.

My life now has purpose, and I am making the impact I feel I was born to make. That is to inspire and motivate millions of Fathers around the world to **TAP**. Having that power tool has turned my life around from a path of FAILURE to a course of VICTORY. Join me and embrace this powerful parenting tool in a world of continuous and fast change.

As I become clear on who I am and build my brand inspired by the great work we do at Brand Builders Club and RippleFEST, I continuously find the courage and gain the knowledge to continue celebrating my daily VICTORY journey. Here I am as a published author in *The Law of Brand Attraction 2* and I continue on this journey of impact and legacy, embracing the raucous ROOOAAAAAR every step of the way!

About Daniel Wood

Daniel Wood is an International Speaker, best-selling Author and in-demand Ambassador of the TAP process, *Thoughtfully Activate the Psoas (TAP)* a life life-transformational transforming process that releases the tension from your body's core to free you from past stress and trauma on every level.

Daniel is on a mission to inspire and motivate fathers to embrace the TAP practice, equipping them with simple tools they can use to give themselves and their children an easy way to reduce the impact of stress and trauma on their bodies. Daniel's own transformation, followed by that of his own children has enabled him to create a VICTORY that both fathers and their children can be proud of.

Having worked with this process since 2012 on his own life and shared the practice with many thousands of people internationally, Daniel is now on a mission to show you how you can do it too.

Contact Daniel Wood

Find out more about the TAP process, created by the Total Release Experience® team at:

daniel@treuk.com

www.treuk.com

Facebook: https://www.facebook.com/groups/victorylions

Instagram: @danielwoodalive

LinkedIn: https://www.linkedin.com/in/daniel-wood-treuk

Raise Your Frequency, Raise Your Game

Debra Sofia Magdalene - The Frequency Alchemist

"Everything is frequency! Raise your frequency and create the life of your dreams."

"How far down your list of priorities do you come?" I was stunned into silence. My coach had asked me a question that took me unaware. To my horror, I was number eight - at the bottom of the list!

"Debra, what on earth are you doing? How are you going to make a global impact if you aren't even looking after yourself?" I asked myself in silent reflection. I wasn't happy. I knew that something had to change. I had to change.

Have you ever had a defining moment like this in your life? Well, this was mine.

This defining moment took me on a long journey of self-discovery, and guess what I found after years of learning, a fortune invested in self-development and thousands of miles worldwide to find answers?

When you raise your frequency, you are happy!

Yes, it's that simple. But if raising your frequency is so easy, why isn't everyone doing it?

It comes down to this... if you want to be happy, no matter what curveballs life throws at you, you have to raise your energy frequency. I know it's not rocket science, but we can complicate the simplest things and energy is one of them.

You cannot be consistently sad when you're living at a high frequency. When you raise your vibration, everyone around you benefits. You also speed up how quickly you manifest when you live in a high-vibe way. So, if you want to build a thriving business and attract everything you want and more, increasing your vibe is the way to go!

Thinking about it isn't enough, however. Yes, thoughts become things, but we're living in uncertain times, plagued with mental health issues and fears. Are you absorbing this energy into your own vibrational field?

Fear, anxiety, stress, guilt... they lower your vibration, compromise your immune system, and make you more susceptible to illnesses. If you're surrounded by negative people, always absorbing the news, or you aren't doing things that raise your energy daily, this needs to change if you're going to make a greater impact and build a movement that raises others.

If you aren't sure where to start, here are the **seven steps to raise your vibration,** increase your energy, become a magnet to positivity and experience joy unlike anything you've experienced before. Let's go!

Step 1 - Happiness Comes from Within

Happiness isn't dependent on external conditions and money cannot buy it.

I became conscious of how my body was affected by external stimuli. From watching TV, to reading newspapers, I realised most of it was bad news. I made a conscious choice to stop doing both and noticed how my mental and emotional wellness improved. When you become conscious of your own frequency and notice what affects it, you can make healthier, conscious choices.

Choose happiness.

What do you choose right now?

Step 2 – Let Go!

Your past doesn't equal your future. Release, forgive and move on. Forgiveness is something you do for yourself, not others.

Have you ever felt like you've been wronged? Once, my car broke down and a passer-by helped when I didn't know what to do. It turned out he was a conman who groomed me and started using my credit cards fraudulently. Using my superpowers, I was instrumental in helping the police track him down. He was a serial criminal! He ended up in prison and I got all my money back. Did I hold a grudge? Absolutely not. I was compassionate to his journey and wondered what must have happened in his childhood for him to act this way. I learned that compassion to myself is equally as important as showing compassion for others. I had been given an opportunity to prove beyond doubt that the victim in me was long gone.

Stand strongly in your personal power to raise your vibration.

What or who do you choose to let go of right now?

Step 3 – Watch Your Words

Words are sound frequencies which create emotion.

Be conscious of how you talk to yourself and others.

Who'd have thought peppermint could change your life? I was offered a drop of peppermint essential oil at a yoga show and felt the instant energy hit for over two hours. I was intrigued. My intuition instructed me to buy a set of oils and I became conscious of my self-talk. It was like having two dogs arguing inside my head.

Fido was saying, *Buy the oils right away. This is an opportunity for you. It will work out.* Fang was arguing loudly, *Debra, don't be ridiculous, you owe money. You can't afford it!*

I stopped giving Fang headspace, got out my credit card and invested in a set of oils. I now teach others about essential oils - they are a fabulous way of instantly raising your vibration!

Be conscious of your thoughts for they create your reality.

Step 4 – Physiology and Focus

What you physically do with your body impacts your mood. Focus on the outcome you want.

"Now isn't the time," he said.

"Now's the perfect time" I replied.

It was just my husband and I in the car with no distractions. I knew things hadn't been right in our marriage for some time. I had just been promoted to Executive Director with a big pay rise and he hadn't acknowledged or congratulated me. He'd been distant for weeks.

"You've found another woman haven't you," I declared. I just knew intuitively. He didn't deny it.

"I didn't want to tell you until we got back from our holiday with the kids," he replied.

I was stunned into silence, breathing deeply to calm my emotions and doing my best to hold back the tears. Life would never be the same.

I wondered: What should I do now? How do I choose to respond to this? What do I want to happen?

Don't react – choose your response and focus on the outcome.

Where is your focus right now?

Step 5 – Gratitude

I knew deep down that he was doing me a favour. *Debra, you just need to find an empowering meaning to your husband leaving you for another woman*, I reminded myself. It took two days of digging deep to find the meaning. ***He's set me free. I can now become the person that I'm destined to be.***

I set the intention to go through a divorce without a single argument, be friends and a good role model for our children - and that's exactly what happened. I experienced intense grief on the emotional rollercoaster and through this process, discovered ***the secret power of gratitude.***

Gratitude is the antidote for every single negative emotion.

This one strategy will transform your life and keep you living at your highest frequency.

What do you have to be grateful for right now?

Step 6 – Make Happiness Your Habit

Daily rituals help keep your vibration high.

I am worth it, I love you, and my body is my temple are examples of things I say to myself to reinforce new habits until they become part of my *way of being.*

Eat high-vibration food – alkaline, raw, living food and fresh juices.

Take high-quality supplements.

Drink clean water to keep your body well hydrated.

Hugging releases happy hormones which raise your frequency!

Do what brings you joy.

What rituals and habits will you build into your daily routine to raise your frequency?

Step 7 – Have a Higher Purpose

Find a way to contribute to others and make a difference.

Show love, compassion and kindness to all living things.

This is especially important as you make your greatest impact in the world.

Speaking of compassion, I had two months of quiet time in March 2020 when my ex-husband died. I allowed myself to be still and quiet. A few months later, a friend sent me a video about a high-tech frequency device which I watched, thoroughly intrigued. Despite having no money, I trusted my intuition and used my credit card to invest in one of these devices without hesitation.

The results were too good to keep to myself and as I shared what it was doing for me, family and friends, I started what would become an international business and global movement!

Not only has it brought in multiple income streams, but I now offer Quantum Frequency Sessions with international clients via Zoom, sell devices and support a team of high-vibe independent distributors which generates additional revenue. Frequency medicine has literally changed their lives and mine emotionally, mentally, physically and spiritually.

Everything I do now is aligned to the global movement I'm building that's fulfilling my higher purpose to raise consciousness. At the same time, it's creating a lasting legacy for my children.

What is your higher purpose?

What first step do you commit to taking right now?

My parting advice to you is this... love yourself enough to put yourself at the top of your list. **When you raise your frequency, you'll raise your game.**

About Debra Sofia Magdalene

Debra is an inspirational speaker, author, digital nomad, and one of the *UK's Leading Evolutionaries* according to Source TV. Debra opens transformational doorways for you to raise your frequency to empower yourself to be happy, healthy and wealthy. She does this by returning you home to your innate superhuman blueprint from which you can create the life of your dreams.

Debra brings many years of coaching, training and mentoring, together with extensive experience in entrepreneurship, personal development, business support and training. She has designed and delivered programmes for thousands to support desired outcomes.

Debra is a gifted healer and energy worker who uses cutting-edge frequency technology and other tools with individuals and groups worldwide.

Contact Debra Sofia Magdalene

https://sociatap.com/DebraSofiaMagdalene

https://www.facebook.com/TheFrequencyAlchemist

https://www.linkedin.com/in/debrasofiamagdalene

Become A Conscious S.H.I.F.T. Maker!

Uroš Brezavšček - The Conscious Shift Maker

"Your ability to create your reality was never questionable. What is questionable is whether you are doing it consciously or unconsciously."

Do you believe in coincidences? I don't, especially after a bizarre accident that happened in the garden a few years ago while planting tomatoes. I hurt my foot badly and what made it so bizarre was that it happened on exactly the first anniversary of another accident I'd had after falling off a ladder that collapsed as I was picking cherries. I'd landed flat on my back and was off work for two months. Was it coincidence? If that didn't get my attention, the next thing did!

Out of curiosity, I looked into the meaning of reflexology points on the foot and what I discovered left me speechless. The area around the wound on my foot represented the same area of my back that still hurt from the previous accident. It turns out the Universe will do whatever it can to make you take notice if you ignore the signs. As it happens, I was totally off track and it was letting me know!

After the cherry tree accident, I'd had plenty of time to think about my life. I realised that I felt totally off-course, unfulfilled, doing a meaningless job, far from living an impactful life. I had no idea how to find my purpose or what to do. Back at work, the daily routine kept me busy without time to think about life.

Occasionally, I experienced anxiety as my health deteriorated, which was a big surprise as I ate healthily, cared for my body and exercised daily.

I was so great at pretending life was OK that I neglected all the messages my body was showing me. First came the unpleasant emotions, followed by anxiety and weakening of my health.

It took two accidents on the same day, one year apart, to finally get my attention. I knew if I didn't change, I would be in for a third accident or serious sickness. I had to act now.

Without knowing what I was going to do next, I quit my job. Literally minutes after I told my boss, I received an email with an invitation to train as a heart coherence coach. Bam! It was a sign from the Universe - I was on the right track! The decision brought immediate relief and to the amazement of my doctors, my health improved overnight. I love to work with people and had already studied a great deal about the power of the heart, so I went for it. I learned a lot of scientifically validated techniques to reduce stress and anxiety, increase creativity and even connect with my intuition. I just couldn't work out how to build a business around it.

I was using all of the great techniques I'd learned every day and experienced huge benefits in my life. However, after three years of trying to make it happen on my own, I ran out of money. It was such a costly mistake, because I had no choice but to go back into engineering. Not only did I feel completely defeated that I hadn't succeeded in building my business, I also felt totally humiliated after I got fired in just five days. For a hard-working perfectionist like me, that was a painful experience. However, I realise now that the Universe was at work again.

With the little money I'd earned and living back with my parents, I decided to give myself one last chance to create a meaningful life. I re-read every book, marked anything that seemed important and searched for everything I could on how to create my reality. After two months of research, I found it.

It was so simple that it seemed impossible to have any effect, but it was this... joy!

As I brought more joy and play into my life, things shifted quickly. I was asked to speak at a few events, which was one of my dreams. My mind was blown after I was offered to fulfil my childhood dream of becoming a helicopter pilot - free of charge! Then at a party, an unexpected perfect job offer came my way, working with children to teach them heart coherence through play. I couldn't believe I was literally being paid to play! After a year of playing however, I got the feeling it was time to move on. The Universe agreed, conveniently lowering the programme's budget and the collaboration came to an end. Another coincidence?

Once again, I was clueless about where to go next. However, this time I knew I could trust that the right path would reveal itself and it did. One day I was talking with a friend about the worldwide crisis and suddenly the realisation hit me: Uroš, if you are talking and thinking about it, you are feeding it with your attention and energy. No wonder the crisis cannot stop! Imagine what could happen if humanity started to focus on something that we want to experience instead.

The idea was so exciting that I shared it with another friend who told me, Uroš, it seems you are building a global movement. Again, by listening to my intuition, I was led to the right mentors in The Visionary Hub to help me bring the idea of this movement into reality. The Conscious Shift Maker movement was born!

I believe there is no greater time than now to create a collective shift in global consciousness. It's critical that humanity remembers our purpose of life, the connection we have with the planet, the power we collectively hold to create Heaven on Earth and our ability to co-create a new golden era.

So, how does this relate to you? How can you consciously shift your life to create Heaven on Earth as you build your global movement? After many years of experience and scientific research, I created the signature S.H.I.F.T. system as a reminder for you to come back to whenever you feel yourself going off-track:

STOP

Connect to your life purpose. What's your Higher Self guiding you to do?

HEART

Reconnect with your heart. What is your heart trying to tell you?

INTUITION

Learn to listen to, trust and act upon your intuition. What does it tell you about something you've had on your mind recently?

FEELINGS

Learn to use your emotions as a guidence and to consciously create your reality. Is there something you'd like to change about a situation? Decide on the feelings you want to have about it, consciously take action and notice how it either shifts or is removed from your path.

TRANSFORMATION

Be consistent and create new habits.

Here's how to go deeper into the first step, so you can experience more joy in your day-to-day life:

1. On a blank piece of paper, write down the title MY LIFE and draw a table with three columns across the page. Name them: WHAT, WHY and HOW.
2. In the WHAT column, list all the things you do during a typical day.

3. For each item on the list answer the question WHY you do it and HOW you feel during and after you've done it in the WHY and HOW columns.

4. On a second piece of paper, draw another table with three columns and this time write the title: WHAT I LOVE, with WHAT, WHY and HOW as the column titles.

   Repeat the steps above, this time answering the question: WHAT I love to do (it makes me feel good, energises me, I could do it all day, etc). Again, for each item on the list, answer the questions: WHY you do it and HOW you feel during and after you've done it in the WHY and HOW columns.

5. Look at the HOW column on the MY LIFE table. Identify each line in which you stated you don't feel good. Look at your reasons WHY in those columns. Those statements are connected with values that are not your true values and that's why you feel this way. Now you see it in black and white, you know what you need to change.

6. By looking at your WHY column on the WHAT I LOVE table, you will discover statements that are connected with your true values. These are the things that are taking you towards the life you want. Do more of these things!

Now is the most critical time in history for you to make this change. Why? Because we are slowly killing our planet and to give life back to it we need a critical mass of conscious shift-makers to remember their purpose and truly live it. In other words, based on the One-Hundredth Monkey Effect, when a critical mass of humans remember how to create Heaven in their own lives (peace, prosperity, living in harmony with nature), the rest of humanity will realise it too.

It's time for you to remember your purpose and truly live it. Together, we can create Heaven on Earth – one conscious shift-maker at a time.

About Uroš Brezavšček

Uroš was born with a life-threatening bleeding disorder called hemophilia, which gives him a unique perspective on life. Already in his early teens, he kick-started his spiritual and personal development journey after many hospitalisations and years of pain.

Thanks to his condition, he has first-hand experience of the power of mind-body connection, where his moods and strong emotions led him to spontaneous bleeds and even injuries. He's travelled the world, spoken on global stages and pioneered revolutionary ideas into the bleeding disorder community.

Based on his learnings and experiences over the last 20 years, impossible doesn't exist. To bring this awareness to the public and empower people, he is a writer, speaker, author and coach of both individuals and groups on how to create another reality.

He is founder of the Conscious Shift Maker movement, pioneering a shift in global consciousness to create Heaven on Earth.

Contact Uroš Brezavšček

uros@iamuros.com

https://sociatap.com/urosbrezavscek

Part Five

Own Your LANE

Become The Best Thing That Ever Happened To Your Brand

Now Is The Time To E.L.E.V.A.T.E. Your Success

Gaby Gonzalez - The Brand Elevator

*"The key to success is not should I or can I,
but rather elevate yourself and go for it."*

I loathe wasting time and effort, and I spent a lot of time trying to understand why people were more successful than me. I exhausted years convincing myself that they had something different to me, that I lacked the X-factor and I struggled to comprehend how I should kick-start my dream. What I forced myself to realise was that by remaining honest to myself and staying in my lane, I could focus on what I wanted to be.

Life experience teaches you so much at such a fast pace, it can be dizzying. You owe it to yourself to carve time out of your hectic life, to listen to the signs that it gives you. Listen to yourself, listen to your tribe, recognise what drives you, understand your values and motivators. I love to use the term tribe to describe a group of people who work towards a common goal, lift each other to achieve greatness and support the entrepreneurial hustle. It's not easy to find your tribe but when you do, know that they will elevate you.

The daily grind can often be hard, but as you grow and experience the murky waters of life, please understand that your self-worth is greater than you can ever imagine. Let me say that again - you are greater than you can imagine. This realisation will enable you to believe in yourself. Inspired by my tribe and this new belief, I learned the simplest of all lessons; what makes us the best we can be is our determination, our discipline and our drive.

The easiest way to stifle business growth is through procrastination. As Jonathan Goodwin says, The truth is, tomorrow never comes! The minute you step into your tomorrow, it becomes your today.

Social media has become an essential way of life for small businesses, but never more so than now. How do I reach new and existing customers? How should I position my brand? How can I leverage today's social media trends? As your customers adapt behaviours, you must elevate your brand to meet their expectations today, not tomorrow.

My life has steered me to where I am today, a successful female business owner. However, it is a story no different to that of anybody else. I was born in Los Angeles to Mexican parents, and I now live in London. I've had tremendous ups and horrendous downs, but my tribe always remained by my side to keep me grounded and focused. Many people have touched my life with positivity, but none more influential than my father, Francisco Gonzalez. In my eyes, the man defined hard work and relentless dedication until his dying day in November 2020. Throughout his incredible life, he operated more than five businesses and always managed to make his long days look effortless. No doubt, things were definitely made easier as he enrolled his six children into his workday to learn his craft, but more importantly his work ethic.

I didn't realise at the tender age of 12, but those lifelong lessons which guide me today were instilled through days of working with my father. From delivering tortillas to local villages before school, to serving customers in his general store after my homework was finished, he drilled a mindset into me that I will never forget - I am the best thing that can happen to me.

It is this mantra that I have turned to in recent times to jump-start my own personal brand with a vision of supporting others. The world changed in 2020, and this event made me realise today is the day, not tomorrow. I knew my capability, but putting my best foot forward to achieve my vision was daunting.

I dug deep, looked at life's priorities and shouted out loud, Today is the day that I change my life. I shouted it again and again and I believed. This belief in myself was the catalyst that I needed to take those first steps. But what happens after the first step? Where do I go next?

I knew I had determination and that hard work gets the best out of me, but how would I be able to take what he taught me to the next level and enable me to achieve my dream?

I love social media; I knew it was my passion since my first Myspace post. My values encouraged me to support, educate and elevate people and their businesses. Aha, this is MY lane!

My next challenge: how could I combine my passion and my values in my daily life to build a legacy?

I reflected on what I knew so well - Francisco's many businesses. I questioned myself as to how he could have elevated any one of his ventures. I used what life experience had garnered and looked at his businesses from seven different angles. There it was: a method to take an idea, a dream or an existing opportunity to the next level, to elevate it to its rightful place. The E.L.E.V.A.T.E. method was born out of a desire to make me the best thing that happened to me.

I scrutinised my online media agency, broke it down to its bare bones and effectively ripped it apart. I looked at it from a customer's point of view, then a competitor's, a collaborator's and then myself as an owner, ensuring my values are front and centre. I mapped out the seven steps of the method and found that I wasn't being the best thing that happened to my brand, I was far from it. I had a brand, but I wasn't elevating myself, or anybody associated with it. It was difficult, emotional and tiring while at the same time liberating; working to improve myself to the point where I can say I feel I'm being my best self.

How did I do it? Here's how...

Engage In The Right Social Media Channels

- Identify and personalise your social media platforms to target your ideal customers.
- Create a colour pallet, logo, hashtags and a template that fits your brand.
- Design your social media blueprint.

Learn Where To Find Your Target Customers

- Become your customer. How and where would you look for what you provide?
- Conduct research, identify similar brands and spot the latest trends.
- Leverage what exists, bring key learnings into your mindset and apply it to your brand.

Educate Your Tribe

- Educate, share knowledge and make your audience part of you and your brand.
- Offer advice, share tips and produce content such as tutorials, polls, carousels and videos.
- Encourage your tribe to work with you and understand what connects you with them.

Visibility Is Key

- What do you need to do to be more visible and stand out on social media?
- Create content that drives activeness, engagement and awareness.
- Consistency is key. You may not break the internet overnight, but rigour will increase your reach.

Adopt A Strategy

- What is your strategy today? Is it elevating your brand?
- Realign your goals to your vision.
- Develop a social media execution plan.

Team Up With Like-Minded Entrepreneurs

- Collaboration encourages growth. Get to know your like-minded entrepreneurs.
- Identify opportunities to work together and share the mutual benefit.
- Never stop learning about your market, your tribe or yourself.

Evolve Your Brand

- Stagnation will cripple your progress. If you do the same thing every day, you will get the same results every day.
- Analyse the insights and learn from your tribe's interactions with you.
- Understand the impact of a change but be brave to introduce conscious change.

If you want to move your online social media presence from OK to outstanding, take this method to get in your lane, apply it to your brand and then validate, *Are you the best thing that happened to your brand?*

What I have shown you is that no secret formula exits, rather work consistently, engage with your audience, believe in your values and yourself. If all else fails, do as Nancy Naigle says, *Live your life in such a way that when your feet hit the floor in the morning, Satan shudders and says, Oh sh*t, she's awake!*

Days will not go to plan. You may self-sabotage your thoughts. Getting out of bed might be the hardest battle of your day. All of those things are OK. There will be times when you don't succeed, but as long as you learn from failure, then it isn't really a failure, but a learning opportunity.

At the end of the day, you owe it to yourself to ask if you made yourself proud or if your accomplishments today are worthy of your effort. If you're unsure, don't worry, as tomorrow will soon be today and off you go again!

About Gaby Gonzalez

Gaby Gonzalez is CEO of Splash Trends Agency, a fast-growing social media company that supports small businesses and influencers to jump-start their online strategy, build their tribe and elevate their brand. Her mission is to empower entrepreneurs to start leveraging social media with confidence so they can achieve their dreams and create their own success stories.

Originally from Los Angeles and now living in London, Gaby started her career as a Director of Education which sparked her passion to leverage relationships from influencers to celebrities to make a positive change. Through the power of social media, her vision is to teach you how to build your brand online and expand your global reach. A world traveller, Gaby is proof that using the E.L.E.V.A.T.E. method will allow you to be the best thing that happened to you.

Contact Gaby Gonzalez

splashtrendsagency@gmail.com

www.splashtrendsagency.com

Facebook: @Splash.Trends.Agency

Instagram: @Splash.Trends.Agency

LinkedIn: Splash Trends Agency

Twitter: @SplashTrendsUK

Create The Perfect Storm Around Your Brand Own Your Own Lane, Then Hit The Gas

Kay Storey - The Brandstormer

"Stop kicking the can kid, you've got this!"

I became a designer because I can't sing - tone deaf to be more accurate.

As a small child, I remember that dreaded time of year - school choir rehearsals, entering the school hall, standing in line, and shuffling my way towards the piano with trepidation. The twinset, tweed-clad music teacher with calves like a rugby player, would plinky-plonk her way up those keys with purpose, and without exception, when your Mary Jane's inched up to that piano leg, you had to work your vocal magic to her tune.

If you received what I called the *hand of shame* on your shoulder during practice, that meant you had to mime. Guess who was familiar with that!

I remember being invited to remove myself from the said hall and create the designs for the posters because I clearly couldn't sing! Turns out I aced those bad boys and there it is - my first memory of being a designer and owning my lane.

That intrinsic love of colour, design and creation never left me throughout school, college and higher education, where I graduated in Graphic Communications and was launched wide-eyed into the business world.

What I've also known from a very young age is that I'm unemployable. I made it impossible for my bosses. Memories of my first jobs include: counting out penny sweets into bags in the local shop after school while dreaming of better things, (I may have eaten a few), selling ladies knickers on a market stall (I was always late, I'm no early bird), to Saturday's playing poker in a gatehouse with a retired para at a stately home (we'd short change really rude visitors by a few pence and buy an ice-cream with their money at the gift shop, FYI: Geoff always had Strawberry Cornetto). Even an amazing design role after graduating had me taking detours to work after only three months, as I'd already become bored of the journey.

You get the picture. I have always had a problem conforming - I'm a free spirit at heart. Are you unemployable too? I think we'd get on famously. I'll love your free-spiritedness.

I've only ever had four short 'proper jobs', over four years combined, and was made redundant from them all. After my fourth employment dumping, I promised myself that I would never rely on anyone else for my wages again. I'm still keeping that promise: I'm no quitter!

At the ripe old age of 24, I welcomed the freelance years with open arms, and I can tell you they were lots of fun! I worked for lots of different design and branding agencies, working on clients over many different sectors, from small businesses to corporates. Here's the thing: being a designer working in corporate, you are massively restricted, and I needed to be free - to be as creative as I could possibly be, so I shifted my focus and created an agency model business. I found a real passion for helping business leaders and small business owners like you to create incredible brands that look sound different, feel individual and look unique.

I often hear (and it drives me mad) that brilliant business

owners think branding is just for the *big* fish. This is limited thinking if you want your business to grow and thrive. Many people think branding is just a pretty logo, but it's so much more and I will come back to that later.

First, let's talk about the branding process, as you can easily burn through time and money quickly when working with the wrong design team. All too often, I hear of people being ripped off or left broke and broken by receiving poor advice and services. So if you ever find yourself self-doubting or you don't know where to start, don't worry. We've all been there and dipped our toe in that pool. You simply need trustworthy advice and guidance with the branding process, and this will ease any overwhelm you are feeling, giving you more time to do what you do best.

Remember the saying: *You don't get a second chance to make a first impression.* This is so true.

Visualise with me... you are red carpet ready, dressed to impress and you are feeling like the King or Queen of the ball. That's how you should feel when your branding is on point. Not having a great brand identity could be all that's holding you back from your success.

Are you channeling your inner Picasso? Maybe you don't feel creative enough to build a brand that others will love? You're not alone, and this is something I hear all too often. Well guess what? We all have a creative streak in us, and maybe you're just missing the right person to bring that out of you to fire up your right brain. Let's spark some of that creativity in you right now!

1. You Can't See The Label From Inside The Bottle

Everyone, including myself, little Miss Brandstormer, needs another set of eyes on your business from outside, to see the gaps you can't see, to help you grow. A good place to start is to look at your brand from the fresh perspective of your ideal customer. Do you have a team or a mentor that you can bounce your business ideas around with?

Activity: *Name three people you can reach out to over the next seven days to evaluate your ideas and existing branding from a customer perspective. Let's see what you create when you Brandstorm together!*

2. Consistency

If you don't know what you are doing, keeping your brand consistent can feel like trying to herd cats. By maintaining consistency throughout your branding, it reinforces the know, like and trust factor, and ultimately creates brand recognition. We all want a slice of that pie!

Activity: *Are your fonts, images and colours consistent across all of your social media profiles and website?*

3. Ring My Uncle Alan For Branding SOS

I'm not even joking. A common mistake I see is small businesses asking for advice from people who don't know a Scooby-Doo about branding - it's crazy! Posting four terrible variants of a logo they've paid £3.50 for and getting people to vote on their favourite is not going to work! They all usually look like they've been covered in honey and smashed into a bag of skittles. So yes, you may as well ring my Uncle Alan for branding advice - I'm sure he'd enjoy the chat about coffee and cats. If you're serious about your brand being on point, then for heaven's sake, ask an expert - there's plenty of Branders who will happily point you in the right direction. If in doubt, contact me!

Activity: *Find a resource you can trust to learn practical and easy-to-follow branding advice. Feel free to check out the School of Brand Facebook and Instagram pages where I regularly post ideas, advice and musings that will support you to get your branding right first time.*

4. Don't Turn The Gas Off Halfway Through Baking A Cake

When it comes to baking your Brand, there are processes to follow. If you're going to spend time cooking up your Brandstorm, inviting people to dine, the last thing you would do is turn the gas off halfway through baking! By cutting corners, you end up going round in circles and you won't get the results that you want or need.

Activity: *Can you identify any areas in your business where you have cut corners? Can you see how this has/is impacting your success? If so, how?*

5. Are You Keen To Ride The Magical Unicorn To Brand Land?

Perhaps you think there's a fast track to success. Spoiler alert - it doesn't exist! You will find yourself sitting on a donkey called Dave with a cone on its head.

There's an ordered process to follow:

- Brand
- Branding
- Marketing
- Sales

Building your business and brand requires an investment in both your time and money.

Activity:

Are you clear on your vision, mission and values?

Are these reflected in your branding? Eg, your logo, website, social media, online presence, etc.

Do you have a plan for your marketing?

Do you have a plan to generate sales?

Remember this: nobody knows your business better than you - it's your creation. There's only one you and you are amazing!

With the right help and foundations in place, you can establish a brand that's unmistakably you and a business that people believe in.

About Kay Storey

Kay is The Brandstormer, global branding educator, published author and CEO, Founder and Trailblazer behind Brandstorm Creative and School of Brand.

Having spent over 20 years in design and branding with her own business (formerly KDesign), Kay's mission is to elevate brands by creating relevant identities and consistent graphic communications that stand out from the crowd, and visually connect with your audience. Her passion is helping small businesses grow and thrive. Brand identity is an important part of this.

As the saying goes, you never get a second chance to make a first impression. Kay looks at brands from the inside out, considering all the pieces of the puzzle that makes your amazing business your business and understands what it is that makes you, you, to ensure that you are supremely positioned in your field.

Contact Kay Storey

To find out more about how she can help you and your business shine, visit *contactKay.me*

Empowered Life = Empowered Business

Lorraine Crookes - The Sexual Empowerment Liberator

"When you're liberated in life, you're liberated in business."

It was dark by the time I arrived home from work. I did what had now become my usual evening routine of unloading the numerous boxes of paperwork from my car and retiring to the back doorstep to contemplate and cry. With head in hands, I sobbed uncontrollably. I felt broken, confused and alone. There was a darkness deep in my stomach that scared me. I had so much to be grateful for, but aspects of my life were becoming unmanageable.

I was a mum, daughter, teacher and volunteer with a secret life surrounded by stigma, taboo and misunderstanding. The possible humiliation if my family or work found out was literally crippling me with irritable bowel syndrome, migraines and now mild alopecia. My life felt out of control.

With tears streaming down my face, I reflected on my amazing family, incredible friends and awesome career as a middle leader in a secondary school. I was blessed to lead two remarkable teams and my passion for teaching produced life-changing results for all my students. I organised and supported students on residentials volunteering in the holidays. I embraced personal development for work, and for fun I embarked on exciting challenges like charity mountain climbs and teaching in Africa.

Why did I feel so emotionally crippled when everything on the outside looked great? Why was my body crying with dis-ease and pain? Why did my life feel out of control? As my thoughts turned dark with possible solutions, I suddenly heard a voice asking, *What does your soul truly want?*

Have you ever had a moment at a metaphorical crossroads like this, not sure which way to turn? Well, I was at exactly this place and the answer was buried deep in my secret life. A life that gave me freedom, empowerment and connection, but also harboured deep aching shame, guilt and fear. A life that gave me everything for my soul but risked everything important to me.

It was a secret life of swinging, fetish and kink. My curiosity around my sexuality, sensuality and sexual energy had for two decades taken me on an exciting journey of sexual self-discovery and exploration. I loved the adventure, meeting new people, the freedom to be me, the connections and the risk. Like most people, my sexual experiences unravelled by trial and error, but I had embraced a life of swinging, fetish and kink in private meet-ups, swinging parties and clubs. I met truly amazing and inspiring people, had hundreds of incredible experiences and loved everything about my secret life. It was the home of my heart and a place I could be me.

But I was ashamed and scared. It was the complete opposite to my upbringing, my advancing career and how most people in my life viewed me. If my family, friends and work found out, I would feel so humiliated, and what about if I lost my career?

My body, heart and soul were at breaking point with the two extremes of my life. I felt so broken and wanted it all to end. I knew every cell of my body was screaming at me that something had to change. I glanced up at the sky. Through floods of tears and a heart full of anguish, I begged and begged the Universe for an answer. *Please, please help me find an answer.* I sat on that step for hours, shaking in fear and frustration. I reached deep into my heart, but everywhere I looked was a dark corner.

I have no idea how long I sat there sobbing, but when the answer came to me, the birds were singing.

It was in a moment, I suddenly realised life was about who we are, not what we do. Societal and cultural expectations had paralysed my thoughts and perceptions for over two decades, crippling me in fear, shame and guilt. This had to stop! In this one moment, changing my thoughts and perception changed my entire reality.

In January 2016, I resigned from my well-established and successful career in teaching. I had no real plans of what I was going to do, but I made myself a firm promise that whatever the next chapter of my life would bring, I'd continue to empower and educate myself and others. It was time to make my impact in the world.

I studied hard, qualifying in massage, mindfulness, Reiki and anything that got my mind and body healthy, my heart in flow, and my life in a better place. I started meditating, reading and I went on to explore tantric massage and other energy work. I met new people and shared about my now not-so-secret life. I found many others with similar struggles around their sexuality and sexual energy who asked for my help.

In 2018, I founded Shelki to support people wanting to discover, explore and evolve into their sexual energy. My signature system, ***Sexual Mastery - Eleven Pillars to Sexual Empowerment,*** educates and supports people to be empowered in their sexuality, sensuality, sexual energy and life. I have supported thousands of people so far by sharing knowledge, skills in tantra, mindfulness and energy work, both one-to-one, in groups and across social media.

I have stopped living the life I thought I should and now live a liberated life in my truth. I have a global movement, supporting others to be empowered in their life. I educate others and provide the support I never had. I get to live my passion and make a huge impact in the world.

There are no more tears on the doorstep!

Never underestimate the impact of your own journey; the impact you can have if you stand in your power and own it. You are a reflection of your business and your business is a reflection of you!

Are you the embodiment of E.M.P.O.W.E.R.M.E.N.T. within your business?

Have a think about these questions:

- *Explore what you love – Are you doing what you love?*
- *Magic is created by pleasure – Do you get pleasure from what you do?*
- *Protect your boundaries – Could you do this better?*
- *Open new doors – Are you building the right relationships?*
- *Wholeness body balance – How are finding good balance in all you do?*
- *Expression of self – Are you truly aligned to YOU?*
- *Reflect on your journey - Where in your past are the tools to your future?*
- *Mindfulness creates growth – Are you present enough in each moment?*
- *Energy is everything – Where is your energy going?*
- *Nurture you, nurture your business – What do you do for you?*
- *Transform inside to expand outside – Where are you being, rather than doing?*

You can ask these same questions for your intimacy and your family life.

Being empowered and liberated in your own personal life is the best gift you will ever give your business. It doesn't matter what your business is, or who it serves.

If you truly connect with yourself and your individual truth, your business will make the greatest impact it was born to make.

The crossroads will vanish to create a solid path for your future. There will be no more tears on the doorstep, no begging the Universe for answers, no more ill health, no more breaking points or darkness, and no more fear or frustration. When you surrender to understanding your own journey, you don't have to pretend to do business, it just happens - and you get to be the change you want to see in the world.

You are your business, therefore when you're liberated in life, you're liberated in business.

About Lorraine Crookes

Lorraine Crookes is an international speaker, best-selling author, CEO of Shelki and creator of Sexual Empowerment Mastery; the World's most empowering sexual energy programme, giving voice, visibility and connection to sexual energy.

A qualified practitioner in multiple holistic and healing practices, Lorraine is best known as The Sexual Empowerment Liberator. A much sought-after expert in her field, Lorraine has liberated thousands of people to connect to their sexual energy and celebrate who they are, profoundly changing their lives. She has transformed the lives of people struggling with poor mental health, challenging relationships, body trauma, abuse, medical conditions and sexuality.

She is now inspiring a global movement to give millions of people around the world a voice, standing in their truth and celebrating their sexual energy.

Contact Lorraine Crookes

Info@shelki.com

www.shelki.com

www.facebook.com/groups/sedhub

Isn't It About Time You Owned Your Lane?

Carol Vincie - The Performance CO-Pilot

"Your passion generates the energy, excitement, courage and commitment to create your dreams."

I had the pleasure of being in a conference that Mr Wonderful, Kevin O'Leary from the US TV series Shark Tank, was presenting at. All three investments made that day were with women-owned and run businesses. Kevin stated, *I consistently make more money when I invest in women-run businesses. Women are committed to making their businesses work. Most guys will throw something up against the wall. If it works fine, great. If not, they're on to their next business venture.*

This is a message that demands more exposure. Success is not instant soup and building a global movement requires you to tap into your gifts and talents on a consistent basis – no matter who you are. So, what do you do if you aren't quite sure what your gifts and talents are? What do you do if you know what they are, but you aren't spending your time owning them?

Millions of people are born without any financial resources, yet become millionaires, multi-millionaires and billionaires in their lifetimes. They work and create opportunities for themselves and others with the same two gifts that you already have within you: a brain, and the will to succeed by providing value to your dream customers!

Oprah Winfrey – the all-time Queen of Media once said, *I don't think of myself as a poor, deprived ghetto girl who made good. I think of myself as somebody who from an early age, knew I was responsible for myself and I had to make good.*

Howard Schultz – founder of Starbucks, grew up on the wrong side of the tracks in a housing project in Brooklyn, New York. He got 217 rejections when attempting to raise money for the expansion of his coffee shops. His attitude about health, wages, and tuition reimbursements for all employees dates back to the days when his dad was injured on the job and received no benefits.

JK Rowling of Harry Potter fame, wrote in a café because she didn't have an office. Her published once told her, *Find a day job.*

Can you imagine what the world would be like now without these incredibly gifted visionaries owning their lane, believing in their gift and pushing through until they saw their vision become a household name? Their success has inspired millions of other visionaries around the world to courageously go for their dreams, and now it's your turn to switch on your impact tap.

I believe right down to my toenails, that you already have the gifts, talents and magic inside you to change the world. But if there's something holding you back from making your greatest impact, it's important that we find out what that is so you can take your foot off the brake and start accelerating. If you are not living each day intentionally using your gifts and talents to grow your business, this needs to change urgently.

Have you ever heard the expression *Follow your dream and the money will follow?*

As a child, we imagine ourselves in many different roles. What did you want to be when you grew up?

At one time I imagined myself as a fighter pilot – a real stretch of the imagination since any pilot at that time was male.

Then I discovered I didn't handle heights well. It turns out that a symptom of ADD (Attention Deficit Disorder) is poor balance. Even a five-foot ladder is out of my comfort zone!

The first sign of dyslexia affecting my career was my inability to navigate early-stage programming languages with their left-to-right and right-to-left demands. I stumbled upon my gift by accident with the combination of a complimentary letter from a challenging office client and a project that overran, leaving the first choice for an assignment open.

I excelled at project design work and became the go-to expert in converting the business demands of clients into a language that engineers and programmers could turn into products. Those products generated huge amounts of revenue in the information technology world. While this is easy for me as one of my gifts, it appears to baffle the majority of people.

While I stumbled upon my gifts and talents, you don't have to wait to stumble upon yours. I don't want you to depend on chance to uncover your talents, gifts and magic. I want you to build your business with ease and confidence.

The beautiful thing about living at such a time as this, is there is no longer a limitation in how you share your gifts with the world. Technology has made it possible for every small business to look big, even if they are starting out in their basements.

No matter what stage you are at in your business journey, it's one thing to get in lane, and it's really another to stay in it. It's important to keep checking in with yourself to make sure you are still doing the things that make you happy, keep you in lane, and consistently keep you performing at the top of your game.

If I have found myself going off-track, there's an activity that I always find really useful to get me back in lane and therefore, back into my gift.

Perhaps you can give it a go now too...

List the three things you loved in your last five jobs, roles or volunteer activities:

1.
2.
3.
4.
5.

Now list the three things you hated in your last five jobs, roles or volunteer activities:

1.
2.
3.
4.
5.

Once you have written down your answers, take a good look at them. What do you see?

Are there things you have written in the first part of this exercise that you really loved doing but don't get enough time to do now?

Have you written things in the second part of this exercise that you really hated doing, yet you've found yourself still doing those things now on a consistent basis?

What are your above answers really telling you?

When I did this activity again recently, I discovered that my lists were consistent right back to my earliest recollections. My second list was full of things I hated to do, which made it easy for me to know what to avoid! Yes, the world does demand a significant quantity of dull, boring, repetitive tasks - I just make sure I am not the one assigned to those activities anymore!

In knowing what you don't want, it can reveal a lot about the things that give you joy, and let's face it, if it's something you enjoy doing and you find it easy to do, then it's most likely one of your gifts. If it's something you don't enjoy doing, then it's taking you away from being in your gift, which is costing you time and money.

The minute you stop using your gifts and talents on a consistent basis, you will find yourself quickly going out of flow and going out of your lane fast. You will get easily distracted, sidetracked and your productivity will go downhill completely! Sound familiar?

Stay in your gift however, and you are more likely to stay in lane, enjoying all the benefits that a highly productive, high-achieving visionary business owner experiences when in flow.

One thing I know for sure is that it doesn't matter whether you have 90 years, 90 days or 90 minutes left in your life. You don't have an expiration day. You don't know when it will end. But you are entitled to live the most productive, effective, joyous life that you can.

Always remember, your passion generates the energy, excitement, courage and commitment to create your dreams, so go for it and keep your eyes on the prize!

About Carol Vincie

Carol Vincie is an international author, speaker and founder of Productivity Tools & Insights, LLC.

Having enjoyed a highly successful corporate career in the fast-paced, challenging, high-growth information technology field, she managed 60-hour work weeks whilst founding her company on the side.

Her ability to understand process enabled her to navigate multiple industries including: brokerage; banking; insurance – property and casualty, and health care; and engineering, to name a few. In her corporate roles, she was the contact person who passed the clients' business demands for products along to the engineering and programming staffs for implementation.

Carol's strengths include out of the box thinking, critical listening, unique solutions, and candid feedback. These skills, combined with her trail blazing leadership make her the person you and your team need if you want to accelerate your growth.

She has worked in the venture capital arena building teams and making connections with investors and main street businesses to build teams for stability and growth.

Contact Details:

sociatap.com/UncoverYourGifts

From Zero Visibility To Hero Credibility - How To Transform Your Brand Into A Global Movement!

Mark Stephen Pooler - The Global Profile Builder

"No matter your past or present circumstances, you can create any future reality you desire. Success leaves footprints and when looking back you should see a lot of steps!"

You can feel that calling inside you. Your inner knowing is telling you that you were put on this planet for greater things. You have read all the chapters in this book and you are now on fire… armed with tools, strategies and advice to turn your inner game into your outer game. Now it's time to own your lane, step up and own who you are with the brilliance of PR!

Mark, I know PR means Public Relations, but what does that actually mean? you ask.

The best way to describe PR is to understand the difference between *brand, branding, marketing* and *PR.*

Look at this this way...

Your clients are saying you're great. *That's brand.*

You are saying you're great. *That's branding.*

Your adverts and social media posts are saying you're great. *That's marketing.*

Celebrities, press, media and TV are saying you are great. *That's PR.*

PR will give your brand massive exposure to your dream customers through powerful endorsements, such as celebrity endorsements, brand endorsements from big-name brands, and credibility endorsements from businesses that have already built their reputation.

Let's briefly discuss what PR *is not...*

If you're saying things like, I want to get 30 people signed up to my webinar, what you really want is advertising and a direct sales strategy, not PR. You need to run Facebook ads, perhaps even a YouTube campaign, or simply pick up the phone and start calling your prospects to turn direct conversions into customers.

If, however you say, *Mark, I want to build big exposure around my brand or product. I want my credibility, authority and influence to be showing up everywhere,* I'd say *let's talk,* because you're focused on building long-term trust. Trust will always lead to attracting more clients sustainably over a longer time and that's why PR works to build trust around your brand 100% of the time.

Everything you invest in PR will last, whereas the moment you switch off your advert, you'll disappear without trace. PR will always be a great investment of your time, money and energy… when you do it right.

How do you do it right then Mark? I'm so glad you asked!

Keep it simple. Ask yourself what your aim is for every PR article you write. If it's a press release to announce the launch of your new product, for example, your goal could be to attract more high-quality customers to your business, to build brand awareness around it, or establish yourself as an industry leader, but it wouldn't be all three.

Knowing your PR outcome is essential, so answer these questions to maximise the global visibility of every Press Release:

1. What ONE thing do you specifically want your Press Release to achieve?

Circle your answer:

- Build brand awareness and recognition as the industry leader in my niche
- Attract more customers
- Influence more potential customers to visit and talk about your business
- Build trust, credibility and a greater relationship with your target audience
- Generate investor interest
- Spotlight a client case study / good news story (social proof)
- Create controversy around your topic of expertise

2. Who is your target audience, specifically?

Knowing exactly who your publicity is aimed at enables you to quickly identify the perfect press, media and publications for that audience. Think about a customer you already love that needs your help more than ever. Call their face to mind now, then answer these questions:

- What is their age?
- What is their gender?
- What is their marital status?
- What level of education have they achieved?

- Does this person have children and if so, what age are they?
- What are their passions and hobbies?
- Where do they get their information?
  Specifically, which newspapers, blogs, books, apps, social media channels, radio, online/offline, etc.

3. What is your current position in the marketplace?

- What is your competitive advantage / unique selling point?
- What are you doing that your competition isn't?
- What can you provide that your industry doesn't yet?

Answering these questions is a great start toward taking the right steps in the right direction.

Something else to consider is... do you have a controversial story to share? Is there something that's really trending in the news that you can speak about? If you have a worthy story that the world needs to know, you'll do well with PR and media.

One final thing to consider is that as a coach, mentor, consultant or professional speaker, you don't have to wait until you've got a product - *you* are the product. *Your message* is the product. Don't wait to start getting your name out there through PR. Start now!

The more credibility you build, the more calls you'll get when somebody is looking for an expert on their radio interview, news channel, podcast or stage. They'll immediately 'Google' you to see who you are, how you're showing up and how popular you are. They'll be looking to align their brand with influencers who have a following, because they want people on their show that make them look good and add new subscribers to their list. With or without a product, the greater your brand footprint, the greater you can demonstrate truly owning your lane = the more your phone will ring!

I'm just starting out though Mark, is it really possible to go from zero visibility to hero credibility?

Seriously, if I can do it, you can do it!

I come from a past of bullying and severe drug addiction. I was so filled with stress, anxiety and depression that I got into the wrong crowd. I was living a bad life and after an accidental drug overdose at just 21 years old, I collapsed and died. I will be forever grateful to the paramedic team that saved my life.

It was decision time.

Actively change my life or die trying.

I went into the celebrity hair styling industry and by the age of 30, I'd had enough of making lots of money for other people.

It was time to start my entrepreneurial journey, so I left the salons behind to set up as a mobile hairdresser. I later joined a network marketing company, which was brilliant because that opened me up to the world of personal development, self-improvement and mindset. I built a team of fifty business builders in six countries through that company and learned great visibility skills, but I knew I wasn't following my passion.

Something was still missing.

I started going to conferences and events, watching the speakers share their stories. Being a speaker was calling me. I had no speaking skills, but I wanted to do it and I'd learn how along the way! I made a big decision to leave network marketing and jumped in to become a speaker. I spoke all over the UK to build up my profile experience, and invested in the quality coaches and training I needed, knowing it would all come together.

I launched my first book, which didn't do too well because I didn't really know what I was doing, and I wasn't owning my lane at that point.

By the time I launched my second book, I was totally owning my lane and the results spoke for themselves with a best seller in the UK, USA and Canada. That book got me on stages, radio shows and in relentless media all over the world. Then came a big step... speaking on the same stage with Jack Canfield.

My turning point came after I was interviewed on a radio show, only two years ago. They loved my interview and asked me to co-host a show, giving me access to a press badge in the USA. I fell in love with the world of media and PR. It enabled me to contribute to lots of publications, which led to me launching my own radio show. Just 12 months ago, I set up my own agency alongside my media and PR company, MSP News Global. Joining the Brand Builders Club around eight months ago enabled me to raise my profile, elevating my global brand a lot quicker.

Just imagine where you could be in 12 months from now.

If you are sitting at home wondering how you take that message in your heart and turn it into a global movement, the answer is to just take action! You have the calling burning inside of you. You are experiencing the nudges from the Universe letting you know that you are too big for the small things you are focusing on right now.

It's time for you to stop making someone else rich and step up to the calling that's been prodding you (not so subtly) from a Higher place. It's time to stretch your comfort zone elasticity, so go for it!

What are you waiting for?

About Mark Stephen Pooler

Mark Stephen Pooler is the Founder, Editor in Chief, Media and News Publisher of MSP News Global.

Mark oversees the company's media business, as well as its intersection with global business leaders. Prior to forming MSP News Global in 2020, Mark spent his time as a professional speaker, international best-selling author, radio host, and PR and media specialist.

Mark is also the Founder of TMSP Agency, a premium media and PR agency. Here Mark helps high-profile entrepreneurs share their stories through the use of PR and digital media to become known globally.

When not working with his valued clients, Mark enjoys spending time with Lilly, his four-legged bestie.

Contact Mark Stephen Pooler

www.contactmark.me

Want To Be In Our Next Book?

Join us in the next Law of Brand Attraction book to share your motivational story and inspirational message with the world.

Email *Sammy@OneDropMovement.com* with your 150-word biography and a short (no more than 250 word) overview of the story and the key message you would like to share.

Sammy or a member of her team will be in touch with you to share how you can get involved.

One thing is for sure... if you've got an inspirational story that you believe will support visionary business owners to make more impact and income doing what they love, we want to hear it!

How Do I Find Out More About The Visionary Hub Or Brand Builders Club?

The best way to know whether one of these programmes is your best next step is to join us at our next online Brand Accelerator. We run these programmes live in a private Facebook group during the last week of every month to build your brand at the same time as raising money for charity.

It's a fun five-day programme from Monday to Friday for emerging Ripple Makers on a quest to make a greater ROI (Ripple of Impact) with their business, hence the name RippleFEST Quest!

For more information and to book yourself onto our next program visit *www.RippleFESTQuest.com*

Printed in Great Britain
by Amazon

65519010R00122